"Where Are the Donuts?"

"Where Are the Donuts?"

... And 30 Other Bible-Based Meditations

Series # 6

Roger Ellsworth

Unless otherwise noted, Scripture quotations are taken from the New King James Version®. Copyright © 1982 by Thomas Nelson. Used by permission. All rights reserved.

Copyright © 2018, Roger Ellsworth

All rights reserved. No part of this book may be reproduced, scanned, or distributed in any printed or electronic form without permission.

First Edition: 2018

ISBN: 978-0-9965168-7-7

20180220LSI

Great Writing Publications
www.greatwriting.org
Taylors, SC

www.greatwriting.org

Purpose

My Coffee Cup Meditations are short, easy-to-read, engagingly presented devotions based on the Bible, the Word of God. Each reading takes a single idea or theme and develops it in a thought-provoking way so that you are inspired to consider the greatness of God, the relevance of the good news of the life, death, resurrection, and coming-again of Jesus, and are better equipped for life in this world and well prepared for the world to come.

www.mycoffeecupmeditations.com

https://www.facebook.com/MyCoffeeCupMeditations/

Dedication

To

Michael, Barbara and Katherine Butterfield

About This Book

This book is the result of the labors Roger Ellsworth and the thought he has given to various passages of Scripture over the years. You may read more about Roger on page 141.

We hope you will enjoy these Bible-based meditations. We would love to hear from you, so please send us a note to tell us what you think—which ones you liked most, and how they made a difference in your life or in the life of a family member, friend, or work associate. To reach us online, go to www.mycoffeecupmeditations.com/contact

MY COFFEE-CUP MEDITATIONS

Table of Contents

1 "Where Are the Donuts?" 16
2 Milk and Meat 20
3 A Groom Flat on His Back 24
4 Though Troubles Assail Us 28
5 May I Interrupt? 32
6 Saved, Saved, Saved! 36
7 Saved from. . . ! 40
8 Saved by. . . ! 44
9 Saved for. . . ! 48
10 "I'm" 52
11 The Gospel and Jay Piper 56
12 Charlie Clapp and the Crooked Stick 60
13 Two Ways to Die 64
14 The Church Search 68
15 An Exact Measurement 72
16 Zeal in Religion 76
17 Gospel Feeling 80
18 Strength from the Joy of the LORD 84
19 Praying for the Holy Spirit 88
20 God's Goodness in Revival 92
21 Wise Up, O Men of God 96
22 Bones in the Bible (1) 100
23 Bones in the Bible (2) 104
24 Bones in the Bible (3) 108
25 A Doctor's Surprise 112

26 Goodbye to Glory 116
27 Just Call It What It Is! 120
28 Diving Dagon and His Dense Devotees 124
29 Three Questions with One Answer (1) 128
30 Three Questions with One Answer (2) 132
31 Three Questions with One Answer (3) 136

About the Author 141
The Series 142

The App

www.mycoffeecupmeditations.com

Be sure you get the app!

−1−

From God's Word, the Bible...

More to be desired are they than gold,
Yea, than much fine gold;
Sweeter also than honey and the honeycomb.

How sweet are Your words to my taste,
Sweeter than honey to my mouth!

Your words were found, and I ate them,
And Your word was to me the joy and rejoicing of my heart;
For I am called by Your name,
O LORD God of hosts.

Psalm 19:10; Psalm 119:103; Jeremiah 15:16

"Where Are the Donuts?"

It was our annual Christmas gathering. Our two sons, their wives, and their children were all present. Sylvia had worked long and hard to prepare a sumptuous meal. Turkey, ham, dressing, mashed potatoes, gravy, green beans, corn, sweet potatoes, and homemade bread were on the table. And waiting for us on the dessert table were pecan pie and cherry pie.

When the moment came that we had been eagerly anticipating, we took our seats. As soon as our youngest grandchild, Eramin, was comfortably situated in her high chair, she surveyed the table and asked: "Where are the donuts?"

I love donuts. I could eat them every day. I think I shall die peacefully if I have my Bible in one hand and a donut in the other. But donuts, as wonderful as they are, can't give us the kind of nutrition we need to maintain our physical health and strength. For that we must have meat and potatoes. We need vegetables and fruit.

The Bible uses our physical families to convey spiritual realities. As we are born into an earthly family, so we must be born spiritually. We must be, as Jesus said to Nicodemus, "born again" (John 3:3), and, by the way, we can take no more credit for our spiritual birth than we can for our physical birth (John 1:11-13).

When we are born again, we are "babes in Christ" (1 Cor. 3:1). We don't begin our spiritual lives as full-grown, mature spiritual adults. We must grow. It's fine for babies to be babies, but we don't want them to remain babies. We want them to grow. If in ten years Eramin still prefers donuts over solid food, we shall have reason to be concerned.

The gracious God who gave spiritual life to us has also provided food for our growth. That food is His Word, the Bible. The Bible is marvelous in many, many ways. One of the marvelous things about it is that it is both milk and meat—milk for the spiritual babes and meat for those who have grown and are growing.

The Apostle Peter has a message for "newborn babes." He writes: "… as newborn babes, desire the pure milk of the word, that you may grow thereby, if indeed you have tasted that the Lord is gracious" (1 Peter 2:2-3).

The Apostle Paul, on the other hand, laments the fact that his Corinthian readers hadn't progressed spiritually as much as they should have. He says to them: "And I, brethren, could not speak to you as to spiritual people but as to carnal, as to babes in Christ. I fed you with milk and not with solid food; for until now you were not able to receive it, and even now you are still not able" (1 Cor. 3:1-2).

The author of Hebrews observes that his readers appeared to be in a dietary reverse. They had gone from milk to solid food, but now they were going from solid food back to milk. They needed once again to be taught "the first principles of the oracles of God" (Heb. 4:12). He tells them that they were "unskilled in the word of righteousness" (Heb. 4:13).

How do we know if we are making progress in the Christian life? How do we know that we are growing? Paul answers both positively and negatively. On the positive side, we are achieving a greater knowledge of Christ and becoming more like Him. On the negative side, we are no longer "children" who are "tossed to and fro and carried about with every wind of doctrine by the trickery of men..." (Eph. 4:13-14).

Paul is clear. Spiritual growth doesn't mean that we leave behind those doctrines that pertain to the person and work of Christ and go into the deeper truths of the Holy Spirit. The Holy Spirit Himself came to glorify Christ (John 16:13-15), and the more we grow, the more Christ-centered and Christlike we shall be. Those who are growing spiritually don't go around singing, "Less about Jesus." They rather join Eliza E. Hewitt in singing:

> *More about Jesus would I know,*
> *More of His grace to others show;*
> *More of His saving fullness see,*
> *More of His love who died for me.*

-2-

From God's Word, the Bible...

For though by this time you ought to be teachers, you need someone to teach you again the first principles of the oracles of God; and you have come to need milk and not solid food. For everyone who partakes only of milk is unskilled in the word of righteousness, for he is a babe. But solid food belongs to those who are of full age, that is, those who by reason of use have their senses exercised to discern both good and evil.

Therefore, leaving the discussion of the elementary principles of Christ, let us go on to perfection, not laying again the foundation of repentance from dead works and of faith toward God, of the doctrine of baptisms, of laying on of hands, of resurrection of the dead, and of eternal judgment.

Hebrews 5:12-6:2

Milk and Meat

We know the Bible is both milk for spiritual babes and meat for the spiritually mature. We also know that we are not to continue to subsist on the milk of the Word. We're to progress to the meat of the Word.

So we're face to face with an important question: at what point does the Word of God cease to be milk for us and become meat?

I mentioned in the previous reading that some think the milk of the Word has to do with Christ and His salvation, and we are to graduate from those truths to the greater truths of the Spirit. Imagine it! The Christian graduating from Christ!

But the Christian moving from milk to meat is not a matter of leaving certain doctrines behind. It is rather a matter of coming to a greater understanding of those doctrines. It is building on the simple doctrines that we heard when we first accepted Christ.

Doesn't the book of Hebrews tell us to leave "the elementary principles of Christ"? Yes, but this leaving shouldn't be understood in the sense of departing from a place to never return again. It should rather be likened to a man building a house. He lays the foundation, and then he leaves it so he can go on to build on top of it. He doesn't leave the foundation by destroying it or by denying that it is there.

The author of Hebrews was concerned about his readers because, after laying the foundation and starting to build the house, they were acting as if they wanted to destroy the house and the foundation so they could start all over.

These people should have been at the meat level. That means they should have been able to teach others, and they should have been able to discern between true and false teaching (Heb. 5:12-14). But they were back at the milk level—unable to teach and unable to discern.

I was very much at the milk level in the early days of my Christian life. My understanding of salvation was very simple and elemental when I came to Christ. I knew I was a sinner. I knew Jesus was the Savior. I knew I must repent of my sins and trust Jesus as my Savior. I came repenting and believing, and I was saved.

But I didn't stay there. As I read God's Word, read about God's Word, and heard godly men preach, I began to move off the milk level to the meat level. It wasn't that I ceased to be interested in Christ and salvation. Far from it! I became more and more interested in Him and His work of salvation. As I learned, I was amazed at the glories folded into the simple gospel.

For example, if I had been asked as a new Christian to identify the three mediatorial offices of Christ (prophet, priest, and king) and explain each one, I would have been at a loss. With the passing of time, however, I learned about these offices and rejoiced in them.

If I had been asked on the day of my conversion to explain how Jesus could pay for our sin in the six hours He was on the cross, I would have been bewildered.

On the other hand, I was easy prey in those days for those who had mistaken notions about Christ and His redeeming work. I now shake my head in amazement at some of the "teachings" that I simply accepted at face value. One especially comes to mind—that teaching that suggests that God tried first one plan of salvation, then another, then another, and finally decided to send His Son. The truth is God has always had only one plan of salvation, and that plan is His Son.

Am I where I want to be and need to be in the spiritual realm? No. After all these years, I can say with Paul: "Brethren, I do not count myself to have apprehended…" (Phil. 4:13).

When it comes to the deep truths of Christ, there should be an end to the milk, but there will never be an end to the meat. There will always be more to understand, and each new understanding will bring greater wonder and awe.

-3-

From God's Word, the Bible...

"Let us be glad and rejoice and give Him glory, for the marriage of the Lamb has come, and His wife has made herself ready." And to her it was granted to be arrayed in fine linen, clean and bright, for the fine linen is the righteous acts of the saints.
Then he said to me, "Write: 'Blessed are those who are called to the marriage supper of the Lamb!'" And he said to me, "These are the true sayings of God."

Revelation 19:7-9

A Groom Flat on His Back

All was ready. The decorations were in place. The crowd was pouring in. The music was playing. It looked as if it was going to be a beautiful wedding indeed. There was only one problem: the groom was lying flat on his back on the floor in my study. He was sick—really sick. It soon became obvious that he wasn't going to be able to go through the wedding ceremony.

As the minutes ticked away, we became so concerned that we decided to call for an ambulance. While we were waiting for it to arrive, I stood before the audience to tell them that the wedding was canceled because the groom was sick. A wave of laughter rolled across the gathering. They seemed to have immediately assumed that he was merely suffering from wedding-day jitters. So I hastened to add that he was so sick that we had called for an ambulance. A hush fell over the audience as they realized the seriousness of the matter.

When I stepped back into my study, the bride was kneeling beside her groom. "We want you to marry us right now," they said. "You don't want to reschedule?" I asked. "No," was the firm reply, "marry us before the ambulance gets here."

So that's what I did. With the groom lying on his back and his bride kneeling beside him, they exchanged their vows and their rings. I pronounced them to be husband and wife, and seconds later the paramedics arrived and whisked the groom away.

I have seen my share of wedding-day disasters—dropped rings, fainting groomsmen, missed cues, and misbehaving flower girls and ring bearers—but I had never seen anything quite like this. It was my most unusual wedding.

You're wondering about the groom? He spent a day or two in the hospital suffering from acute something or another. The doctors got him on his feet, and he and his bride were off on their honeymoon.

The Bible tells us about some unusual weddings. Jacob thought he was marrying Rachel but woke up the next morning to discover he had actually married her older sister, Leah (Gen. 29:21-30). Samson married a Philistine woman who cried all of the seven days of their wedding feast. The feast ended with Samson calling her a "heifer," and she ended up marrying Samson's best man (Judg. 14:17-20). Jesus attended a wedding feast in which "they ran out of wine" (John 2:3).

The Bible also tells us about a wedding that will take place in heaven. It is the wedding of the Lord Jesus Christ and His bride, the church (Rev. 19:7-9). That's one wedding that will go off without so much as a single hitch. No one will get sick. No one will be late.

I've heard many a bride express her desire for everything to be "perfect" for her wedding. Perfect weddings seldom occur here, but everything will be perfect when Jesus weds His bride. It will be the perfect groom marrying the perfect bride in the perfect place. And the marriage, unlike those of this earth, will be perfectly harmonious and will never end.

How is it that the Lord Jesus Christ has a bride? The Bible says it's because He came to this earth for the express purpose of taking a bride for Himself. But the bride He desired for Himself was not ready for marriage. She was deeply stained by sin. In order for Him to marry her, she had to be made clean. In other words, the penalty for her sin had to be paid. Jesus went to the cross and "gave Himself" for her (Eph. 5:25).

There He stands on the hill of Golgotha. A wooden stake stands behind Him. He is about to be crucified. But He must first be nailed to the crossbeam lying on the ground. So the Roman soldiers hurl Him to the ground and drive those nails into His hands. Here we have another groom lying flat on His back. And that is how this groom happens to have a bride.

> *From heaven He came and sought her*
> *To be His holy bride,*
> *With His own blood He bought her*
> *And for her life He died.*
> (Samuel J. Stone)

−4−

From God's Word, the Bible...

And Abraham called the name of the place,
The-LORD-Will-Provide; as it is said to this day,
"In the Mount of the LORD it shall be provided."

Genesis 22:14

"Though Troubles Assail Us"

John Newton and *Amazing Grace* are almost synonymous. Mention one, and the other comes to mind. It is certainly my favorite among the many hymns he wrote. By the way, it was originally titled *Faith's Review and Expectation*.

One of Newton's lesser-known hymns has the title *Though Troubles Assail Us*. It is a precious hymn, combining a very realistic view of the Christian life with a sturdy confidence that we can trust the Lord to care for us. Each of its four verses ends with the phrase "The Lord will provide."

The hymn, based on Genesis 22:14, asserts that we can depend on God to provide when "troubles assail us and dangers affright" and when friends "all fail us" and "foes all unite."

What a fearful picture! Friends running from us in full flight and all our foes uniting against us!

In the face of these things, Newton fastens our attention

on "one thing." This is the thing that "secures us" no matter what comes our way, and that "one thing" is the assurance that "The Lord will provide."

In the second verse he calls our attention to the birds. They don't have a place to store their food, but yet they are fed because the Lord provides for them. If the Lord cares for birds, shouldn't we trust Him to care for us? (Matt. 6:26).

Newton mentions our foes in verse 1. In verse 3 he identifies our capital Foe. It is none other than Satan himself. He hates the Lord with unsurpassed hatred. Since he can't invade heaven and dethrone God (he tried that and failed before the world was created), he does the next best thing—attacking God's people. He's always trying to "stop up our path," that is, he's always trying to impede our progress in the Christian life. He's such a fierce and devious foe that sometimes "courage all fails us."

But with all his cleverness and subtlety, there are things the devil can't do. One of them is this: he can't take from us the Lord's promise—a "heart-cheering promise" it is—that the Lord will provide. In verse 2, Newton uses the phrase "So long as 'tis written, The Lord will provide."

He's essentially telling us to go back to the Bible to see if the promise is still there. We have reason to fret and worry if we open our Bibles to find that it has been deleted. Imagine us opening our Bibles to find a horrible blank space where once the promise was written! But that can never be! Let's check our Bibles, and we will find the promise still there, and if it's still there we can rest and be at peace. It comes down to this: if the promise isn't there, we're not okay; if it is there, we are okay. When it comes to this promise—or any of God's promises—the delete key on Satan's computer doesn't work.

Looking into the Bible ought to be enough for any child of God, but any Christian who feels in need of any more assurance can, as Newton says in verse 4, look to "the Savior's great name." Do we doubt that the Lord will provide for us? Then let's look to the Savior! On the cross He provided salvation for us. If He made the greatest of all provisions for us, how can we doubt that He will provide for us in every other area of life?

Read now the entire text of Newton's hymn. Read and rejoice!

> *Though troubles assail us and dangers affright,*
> *Though friends should all fail us and foes all unite,*
> *Yet one thing secures us, whatever betide*
> *The promise assures us, The Lord will provide.*
>
> *The birds, without garner or storehouse, are fed;*
> *from them let us learn to trust God for our bread.*
> *His saints what is fitting shall ne'er be denied*
> *So long as 'tis written, The Lord will provide.*
>
> *When Satan assails us to stop up our path,*
> *and courage all fails us, we triumph by faith.*
> *He cannot take from us, though oft he has tried,*
> *this heart-cheering promise, The Lord will provide.*
>
> *No strength of our own and no goodness we claim;*
> *Yet, since we have known of the Savior's great name,*
> *In this our strong tower for safety we hide:*
> *The Lord is our power, The Lord will provide.*

-5-

From God's Word, the Bible...

, . . .and that from childhood you have known the Holy Scriptures, which are able to make you wise for salvation through faith which is in Christ Jesus.

2 Timothy 3:15

May I Interrupt?

I'm beginning to see a trend—a Christmas trend. It has to do with the way many preachers choose to treat the appearances of angels to Joseph (Matt. 1:18-25) and Mary (Luke 1:26-38).

We're told that Joseph and Mary were going about their busy lives and planning for their future, and suddenly these angels appear to interrupt them. What are Joseph and Mary to do? How are they to handle these interruptions?

We're also told that since we have our own interruptions, we're wise to read about Joseph and Mary to find clues for handling them.

It's true that we have interruptions. They're a constant part of life. Many of them are minor in nature. The car breaks down. An unexpected guest drops in. A tooth begins to ache. Junior falls and scrapes his knee as we're rushing out of the house to begin our busy day. Such things can be irritating and frustrating, but do we really need special guidance for dealing with them?

Other interruptions are major. I think of a dear family who a few months ago had their lives interrupted with a diagnosis of cancer for the young husband and father. Their normal way of living has been interrupted and replaced with a new normal.

In my years as a pastor, I had my fair share of both kinds of interruptions. So I certainly don't want to minimize the problem.

If interruptions are a real problem, what's wrong with looking at the appearances of angels to Joseph and Mary through that lens? Didn't those angels interrupt them? Yes. But do we really think Matthew said to himself, "People are having so much trouble with interruptions that they need to learn how Joseph handled his."? Do we really think Luke said the same about Mary?

May I interrupt on this business of interruptions? These passages were penned to point us to something truly glorious—the coming of the Lord Jesus to provide the way of salvation for sinners. To come to them looking for "tips" on how to deal with interruptions is to trivialize them. It's to descend from the high level of redemption to a much lower level. It's to take that which is marvelous and make it mundane.

We most certainly do need help in handling a major interruption (such as a cancer diagnosis), and we can find it by turning to verses that assure us of God's loving care for us, His wise purpose in allowing harsh circumstances to come our way, and His pledge to sustain and strengthen us (Ps. 55:22; Rom. 8:28; 1 Peter 5:7), keeping in mind that even these truths must be seen in light of God's work of redemption.

One of the major developments in "preaching" the last several years is presenting the Bible as a "tips for coping" book instead of what it is—the book in which God graciously reveals His plan for saving sinners through His Son.

With all of our comforts, conveniences, possessions, and leisure, it's somewhat baffling that we find life to be so utterly challenging and difficult that we constantly need tips for the living of it and that we take delight in finding those tips in the Bible. What does it say about us if we glory more in dealing with trivial things than we do in the truly glorious thing? How did we reach this point where the trivial is more glorious to us than the glorious?

If we reconfigure the Christmas stories to make them about handling life, do they have any meaning for those who are handling life very well? Doesn't our reconfiguring give unbelievers a legitimate reason for rejecting Christianity? Can't we hear them saying, "So Christianity is about handling life? No, thanks, I'm handling life quite well."?

The true Christmas message addresses our universal need. We don't all need help handling interruptions, but we are all sinners (Rom. 3:23) in need of a Savior. Christmas tells us that the Savior has come. His name is Jesus (Matt. 1:21). Our most urgent need isn't to learn how to deal with interruptions. It is rather to be interrupted as we speed toward eternity. It is to be so interrupted by the knowledge of our sins and the saving work of Christ that we flee to Him in repentance and faith.

-6-

From God's Word, the Bible...

Happy are you, O Israel!
Who is like you, a people saved by the LORD,
The shield of your help
And the sword of your majesty!
Your enemies shall submit to you,
And you shall tread down their high places.

Deuteronomy 33:29

Saved, Saved, Saved!

Prowl around for a while in the dustbin of old hymns, and you might come across the happy, exuberant selection *Saved, Saved!* This hymn was written by Jack P. Scholfield in 1911. He had this to say about it: "The melody just came to me, almost as a gift. Then I simply tried to make the words fit the tune."

I first got acquainted with this hymn as a child. I remember the congregation in our little country church boisterously singing the chorus:

> *Saved by His power divine,*
> *Saved to new life sublime!*
> *Life now is sweet and my joy is complete,*
> *For I'm saved, saved, saved!*

How those people loved to emphasize in their singing that threefold "saved!" They seemed to me to glory in it, and I can't help but think their robust singing of it must have arrested the attention of unbelievers. It must have caused them to ask: "What is this 'saved' business? What does it mean? Why do these people delight in it so?"

I wonder about unbelievers who might wander into churches today. Picture Unbeliever X. He has about reached the end of his rope. He finds little joy and satisfaction in life. He carries an awful sense of dread as he thinks about death. He has the gnawing intuition that there is a God and that he must ultimately stand before Him. He has heard about Christianity all of his life, but he has always dismissed it, sometimes with a derisive scornfulness. He has always wanted to be considered intelligent and trendy by his friends, and none of them regards Christianity as something intellectuals could possibly embrace. But he can't help but wonder…

So he musters courage one Sunday and decides to give Christianity a try, without, of course, letting any of his friends know.

Do you have a picture of Unbeliever X clearly in mind? Do you see him slipping in a little late and sitting in the back row? Here now is my question: What will going through a church service cause Unbeliever X to say about what we as Christians delight in?

Would he get the impression that we delight in this matter of being "saved"? Would he come away thinking that this is the most wonderful and glorious of all things and that he must have it? Or would he conclude that Christianity is just a way of coping with the various strains and stresses of life? Would he get the impression that Christianity is a way to have "health and wealth," and he doesn't need it because he is already healthy and wealthy?

The saving work of the Lord Jesus Christ ought to be prominently displayed in our churches, but, tragically, it's possible to attend many services these days without hearing much about it. An unsaved person may sit in service after service without getting answers to the three most vital questions that can ever be asked. The first is: *What do I need to be saved from?* The word "saved" means "to be rescued from danger." What is the danger that we need to be rescued from?

A second vital question is: *"What am I saved by?"* When someone is saved from danger, a saving instrument or means is involved. The saving instrument for a drowning person might be a lifeguard. The saving instrument for one in cardiac arrest might be a doctor or nurse. What is the saving instrument for sinners?

And a third vital question is: *"What am I saved for?"* Another way to put it is: "How will being saved change me or how will it affect my life?"

The next three readings will take up each of these questions with a twofold hope. One is that that Unbeliever X will come to understand salvation and will lay hold of it without delay. The other is that those believers who have seen the wonder of salvation fade will get it back to the extent that they can once again sing with great vigor and joy:

Life now is sweet and my joy is complete,
For I'm saved, saved, saved!

As we prepare for the next three readings, let me ask you quite plainly: Are you sure that you have been saved?

– 7 –

From God's Word, the Bible...

Much more then, having now been justified by His blood, we shall be saved from wrath through Him.

For they themselves declare concerning us what manner of entry we had to you, and how you turned to God from idols to serve the living and true God, and to wait for His Son from heaven, whom He raised from the dead, even Jesus who delivers us from the wrath to come.

Romans 5:9; 1 Thessalonians 1:9-10

Saved from...!

The word "saved" is one of the Christian's favorite words. A rich word it is! And I love the threefold "saved" with which the chorus of *Saved, Saved* ends.

I can't tell you what Jack P. Scholfield was thinking when he penned that threefold "Saved." I suspect that he, realizing how very slow God's people can be to apprehend and appreciate their salvation, was simply trying to drive home the wonder of it. But, on the other hand, he might have been thinking that we are saved by God the Father, by God the Son, and by God the Holy Spirit. Or he may have thinking that we are saved by grace, by faith, and by blood, that is, by the blood of Christ. Perhaps he was thinking that we have been saved (justification), we are being saved (sanctification), and we will be saved (glorification).

I can tell you that his threefold "Saved" has made me think about these three questions: What are we saved *from*? What are saved *by*? What are we saved *for*?

These are three questions with one answer, and the answer is God. We are saved from God, by God, and for God.

Saved from God! Can that be right? Isn't it more correct to say we are saved from sin or saved from hell? Yes, thank God, we are saved from sin and from hell, but it's even more fundamentally true to say we're saved from God. More to the point, we are saved from the wrath of God.

Why do we need to be saved from sin? Our sins bring God's wrath upon us! Why do we need to be saved from hell? Hell is the final and ultimate expression of God's wrath.

Many these days either believe that there's no such thing as God's wrath or, if there is, only the very worst people will experience it. But the Bible teaches that because we're all sinners, we all deserve God's wrath. What is sin? It's refusing to live the way God has told us to live. It's refusing to conform to His commandments. Don't look at others to determine whether you're a sinner. Go through the Ten Commandments (Exod. 20:1-17), and let them tell you whether you are a sinner.

Our sins deserve God's wrath, and that wrath is a terrible thing. The book of Hebrews says: "It is a fearful thing to fall into the hands of the living God" (Heb. 10:31). It's no wonder that we are urged to "flee from the wrath to come" (Matt. 3:7).

What terrible terms the Bible uses to describe hell! Weeping, wailing, gnashing of teeth; unquenchable fire; everlasting destruction; flaming fire. Some lightly dismiss these terms as "figurative language." But hell must be a horrible reality indeed to require such figures to describe it.

In these delicate days, many find the wrath of God to be very upsetting. They think it is very uncomplimentary toward God. To suggest God has wrath is, in their view, to insult Him. To them we must either say, "God is love" or "God has wrath." To say one, they argue, is to eliminate the other. But the same Bible that teaches the love of God (John

3:16; 1 John 4:10) prominently emphasizes the wrath of God. Most notable in that emphasis is what Jesus Himself had to say (Matt. 7:13-14; 22:13-14; 23:33; 25:30,41,46; Mark 9:42-49; Luke 16:19-31).

It seems to me to be astoundingly audacious to say that Jesus knew what He was talking about when He stressed the love of God (as in the parable of the prodigal Son—Luke 15), but was completely off base when He stressed the wrath of God! We can't have the Jesus who teaches love without taking the Jesus who teaches wrath.

We will never sing *Saved, Saved!* as triumphantly and joyfully as we should until we realize how horrible is the wrath from which we are saved. Conversely, when we have realized to a large degree the wrath from which we're saved, no one, including the devil himself, will be able to keep us from rejoicing with "joy inexpressible and full of glory" (1 Peter 1:8) in that wonderful word "saved."

-8-

From God's Word, the Bible...

For when we were still without strength, in due time Christ died for the ungodly. For scarcely for a righteous man will one die; yet perhaps for a good man someone would even dare to die. But God demonstrates His own love toward us, in that while we were still sinners, Christ died for us. Much more then, having now been justified by His blood, we shall be saved from wrath through Him. For if when we were enemies we were reconciled to God through the death of His Son, much more, having been reconciled, we shall be saved by His life. And not only that, but we also rejoice in God through our Lord Jesus Christ, through whom we have now received the reconciliation.

Romans 5:6-11

Saved by...!

The chorus of Jack P. Scholfield's hymn *Saved, Saved!* ends with a threefold repetition of that wonderful word "saved." That threefold repetition has spurred me to think about these questions: What are we saved *from*? What are saved *by*? What are we saved *for*?

What wealth we have in those prepositions!

Each of those questions has the same answer: God. We are saved from God, by God and for God. The late R.C. Sproul has this to say about those who are shocked at the thought of being saved from God: "We fail to understand who God is, and we fail to understand who we are. Our view of God is too low, and our view of mankind is too high."

Now we come to the second question: What are we saved *by*? The glorious answer of the gospel is this: The very God *from* whom we need to be saved is the One who saves. We are saved *by* God!

The way in which God saves us from Himself is the death of His Son, Jesus, on the cross. Paul makes this clear in these phrases: "Christ died for the ungodly" (v. 6), "Christ died for us" (v. 8), "by His blood" (v. 9), "through the death of His Son" (v. 10).

Many fail to see the nature of what the Lord Jesus did on the cross. They know He died there for sinners, but if you ask them to explain how His death actually achieves our salvation, they are at a loss. The answer to the question of how Jesus' death actually saves is this: it satisfied God's justice.

God can't simply set aside His justice or His wrath against our sins in order to let us into heaven. He has pronounced the sentence of eternal separation from Himself as the just penalty for our sins. That penalty has to be paid. The only way the sinner can pay is by enduring it, that is, by being eternally separated from God.

But God provided another way for that penalty to be paid. That way is Jesus. He could pay the penalty for others because He had no sin of His own for which to pay. He could pay it for many because as God in human flesh, He was an infinite person. And as an infinite person, He could receive in a finite length of time an infinite amount of wrath.

To describe what Jesus did on the cross, Paul also uses the word "propitiation" (Rom. 3:25). To propitiate someone is to appease or satisfy that person's wrath. On the cross, Jesus satisfied the wrath of God so that all sinners who entrust themselves to what He did there will not have to satisfy that wrath themselves. God's justice demands that the penalty for sin be paid, but it only demands that it be paid once. If God demanded the penalty for sin be paid twice, He would not be just. Since Jesus paid the penalty, all who believe in Him will never have to pay it.

Why did God do this? Why did He put His Son on the

cross to pay the penalty for sinners? Paul answers in these words: "But God demonstrates His own love toward us, in that while we were still sinners, Christ died for us" (v. 8).

It was the love of God that satisfied the wrath of God! If we realize this, we can join Charles Spurgeon in rejoicing over that word "saved":

> Why that word "saved" is enough to make the heart dance as long as life remains. "Saved!" Let us hang out our banners and set the bells a-ringing. Saved! What a sweet sound it is to the man who is wrecked and sees the vessel going down, but at that moment discovers that the lifeboat is near and will rescue him from the sinking ship. To be snatched from devouring fire or saved from fierce disease, just when the turning point has come, and death appears imminent, these also are occasions for crying, "Saved." But to be rescued from sin and hell is a greater salvation still, and demands a louder joy. We will sing it in life and whisper it in death, and chant it throughout eternity — saved by the Lord.[1]

---

[1] Charles Spurgeon, *Metropolitan Tabernacle Pulpit*, Pilgrim Publications, Pasadena, TX, 1983, vol. xxiii, p. 343

-9-

From God's Word, the Bible...

For the grace of God that brings salvation has appeared to all men, teaching us that, denying ungodliness and worldly lusts, we should live soberly, righteously, and godly in the present age, looking for the blessed hope and glorious appearing of our great God and Savior Jesus Christ, who gave Himself for us, that He might redeem us from every lawless deed and purify for Himself His own special people, zealous for good works.

Titus 2:11-14

Saved for...!

Jack P. Scholfield's triple "Saved" has stirred me to think about what we are saved from, by, and for. The answer in each case is God. We are saved from God, by God, and for God.

We've considered the "from" and the "by." Now it's our privilege to consider the "for."

Some people seem to think that God saves us for ourselves, that is, He saves so we can live for ourselves and do what we want to do. In his letter to Titus, the Apostle Paul responds with a resounding "No!" He tells us that God saves us "for Himself" (v. 14). He saves us so we can live for Him and do what He wants us to do.

This is the purpose that God had for Adam and Eve. They were created to live for the honor of God. They were intended to bring pleasure to God. We know what happened—they fell into sin. Instead of living up to God's purpose, they fell short of "the glory of God" (Rom. 3:23).

How the devil and all his minions must have hooted and howled in delight as they viewed Adam and Eve in sin. I can imagine the devil mocking the Lord in this fashion: "You made this man to honor Your name, and look at him! He has done exactly the opposite. He has disgraced You. Your grand effort is a failure. Man was supposed to be a testimony to Your power and wisdom. The proof is in! You aren't so powerful and wise after all. You couldn't even make a man who would do what You wanted him to do."

If that comes close to the mockery hurled at God by the devil, we must say that he, the devil, was in for quite a surprise. The sin of Adam and Eve didn't take God by surprise. It rather gave Him the opportunity to do something that would bring more glory to His name than He would have received if Adam and Eve had never sinned at all.

That "something" was His plan of redeeming sinners through the atoning death of His Son, the Lord Jesus Christ.

When Adam and Eve sinned, the devil may have thought that God would never have a people to honor Him. But the Apostle Paul tells Titus that God's plan of redemption would create for Him "His own special people" (v. 14; see also 1 Peter 2:9-10).

The devil is still in the business of mocking God. He often does his mocking through human instruments. There are skeptics and Christianity-haters in abundance these days. They are eager to say that God's plan of redemption is working no better than His original creation. They gleefully point to Christians and say, "Look at them! They don't bring honor to God! Most of them don't even go to church on the very day God has appointed for them to worship Him! And the way they live is no different from the way unbelievers live."

How are we to respond to such mockery? First, we must candidly admit that we Christians do fail in many ways.

Secondly, we must say that many who profess to be Christians are not. Profession doesn't equal possession! The haters of Christianity either fail to see this distinction, or, seeing it, refuse to acknowledge it. They know that if they once admit that many are not Christians who claim to be so, much of their mockery loses its punch.

Finally, we must respond to the skeptics' mockery by pointing out that God's plan of redemption isn't complete. When it is complete, God will be fully vindicated and glorified. The mouths of the skeptics will be stopped as all of creation joins in this anthem:

> *Blessing and honor and glory and power*
> *Be to Him who sits on the throne,*
> *And to the Lamb forever and ever.*
> (Rev. 5:13)

Saved from, by, and for God! In these days in which we have been, as R.C. Sproul said, "inoculated against amazement," let's ponder anew the vast scope of our salvation and live to the praise of the God who planned it in eternity past, provided it on the cross of Christ, and applies it through the regenerating work of the Holy Spirit.

-10-

From God's Word, the Bible...

This is a faithful saying and worthy of all acceptance, that Christ Jesus came into the world to save sinners, of whom I am chief.

For this reason I also suffer these things; nevertheless I am not ashamed, for I know whom I have believed and am persuaded that He is able to keep what I have committed to Him until that Day.

1 Timothy 1:15; 2 Timothy 1:12

"I'm"

What is the most important word in Jack P. Scholfield's hymn *Saved, Saved!*? Oh, that all questions were so easy to answer! It is, of course, the word "saved." We've given some attention to that word in the last few readings, but we haven't come anywhere near exhausting it. Eternity itself will not exhaust it.

The same hymn contains many other important words: love, grace, power, life, and joy. Volumes have been written about the significance of each of those words in the context of the Lord saving sinners.

The hymn contains one word that could very easily escape our attention. It's a very small word, but a most crucial word. Large doors swing on small hinges!

I'm referring to the contraction "I'm."

"I" is the most personal of all words. It can never refer to anyone except the person who speaks or writes it. And "am" refers to the present. In using it in his chorus, Scholfield is telling us that he is in possession of God's wonderful salvation. It is his right now.

Think about it! A person actually possessing all that is folded up in that word "saved"! Forgiveness for sins, deliverance from the wrath of God, right standing with God, freedom from fear and dread of judgment, title to eternal glory—all of this (and much, much more) belongs in that word "saved," and all of it can actually be possessed here and now by each one of us!

Do you possess it? When it comes to this matter of being saved, can you use the contraction "I'm"? Can you say, "I'm saved."?

As noted, "I" is a personal word. No one else can possess salvation for you. You must possess it for yourself. No one else can say, "I'm saved" for you. You must say it for yourself.

I was immeasurably blessed to have parents who knew the way of salvation, who talked to me about it, and who made sure that I was in a church where it was continually and persuasively presented. But I'm not saved by virtue of having believing parents or by being in that church. My parents could not believe for me, nor could my church. I had to personally lay hold of God's salvation. I had to make it mine. I had to say for myself, "I'm saved!"

There was once a man who was asked about his religious beliefs. He answered by saying: "I believe what my church believes." His questioner then asked: "And what does your church believe?" His answer was: "My church believes what I believe." His questioner was persistent. He next asked: "And what is it that you and your church believe?" The man responded: "We both believe the same thing."

There seems to have been a decisive and definite "I'm" missing in that evasive and elusive man.

What is necessary for a person to say: "I'm saved"? That's what the Philippian jailer wanted to know from Paul and Silas, and Paul was ready with the answer: "Believe on the Lord Jesus Christ, and you will be saved…" (Acts 16:31).

In his letter to the Romans, the same apostle writes: "…whoever calls on the name of the Lord shall be saved" (Rom. 10:13).

Will be saved! Shall be saved! The promise is the same in each of those verses.

Do you want to be saved? Believe and call! Yes, believe the facts about Jesus, but don't stop there. Rest on those facts. Entrust yourself as a sinner to the Lord Jesus who came from heaven to be the Savior for sinners. Renounce every other hope, and depend on what He did for sinners. And call to Him in the words of Simon Peter: "Lord, save me!" (Matt. 14:30) or in the words of the publican: "God be merciful to me a sinner!" (Luke 18:13).

Don't believe partially. Don't call halfheartedly. Believe that you are a sinner and the Lord Jesus saves sinners, and call out to Him to save you. You need not look into the misty counsels of eternity to determine if you are among the chosen. Look to Jesus and be saved.

Believe fully, call fervently, and rejoice with Scholfield in saying, "I'm saved, saved, saved!"

-11-

From God's Word, the Bible...

Therefore, if anyone is in Christ, he is a new creation; old things have passed away; behold, all things have become new.

2 Corinthians 5:17

The Gospel and Jay Piper

Early in his life, Jay Piper became part of a street gang and got into so much trouble that it was either go to jail or go to the Marines. He chose the Marines.

Jay wasn't sure what he wanted to do with his life when his tour of duty with the Marines ended, but he was sure that he wanted nothing to do with Christianity. He was a sin-hardened young man, drinking heavily, cursing freely, and living immorally. There weren't many evils that he hadn't already experienced.

The day Jay returned from the Marines brought a cloud of darkness across his sky. His sister, a devoted Christian, wanted him to go to church with her. Revival services were being conducted that week at her church, and, yearning for him to hear the gospel, she asked him to attend one service. Jay hated church, but he loved his sister. So he told her he would go one time, but only one. That very night they went to church.

The preacher's sermon was essentially divided into two parts—bad news and good news. The bad news is that we are all sinners. We have all violated God's laws time after time in spirit and in deed. There was more. The God whose laws we have broken doesn't take our sinfulness lightly. A great day of judgment is coming in which we will all stand before God to give account of ourselves. If we stand before Him in our sins, we will be driven from Him forever.

As Jay listened to these things, he was infuriated. Almost every word angered him. It seemed that the preacher knew all about him and was preaching directly to him. He became so angry that he promised himself that he would confront the preacher after the service and beat him up.

Suddenly the preacher turned to the second part of his sermon—the good news. The very God who hates sin and promises judgment loves sinners. Because of that love He sent His own Son, Jesus, into this world to live the kind of life God demands of us, the life of perfect obedience to His law. After living that perfect life, Jesus died on the cross a special kind of death, one in which He actually received the wrath of God in the place of sinners. God now calls all sinners to repent of their sins and to believe in the Lord Jesus.

Christianity is this: Jesus got the penalty our sins deserve, and we get the righteousness He provided by His life.

Jay never got to beat up the preacher. The Spirit of God laid hold of him, granted him repentance, and enabled him to believe the gospel.

When Jay arrived home that night, it was not long before he became aware that he was a new creature in Christ. He went to the fridge to get a beer, but after taking a couple of sips, poured it out along with all of his other beers. The power of this thing that had long enslaved him was now broken by the far greater power of God, as Jay realized that he couldn't go on living as he had before.

It wasn't long until the Spirit of God was dealing with him again—this time about preaching the gospel. Jay answered that call and faithfully preached Christ until God called him home in 1983. He was only forty-two years of age.

So Jay Piper went from hater to herald—from hating the gospel of Christ to heralding it.

I know these things because Jay Piper was my dear friend. I heard him share his experience of God's saving grace many times, and each hearing of it brought joy to my heart.

Jay's soul has now been with the Lord for many years, and his body will be raised from the grave when Jesus comes (1 Thess. 4:13-18). I look forward to seeing him again, and I look forward to hearing him glorify once again the gospel that made him a new creature in Christ. I hope he will give me a few minutes to add my own testimony about that glorious, saving gospel.

-12-

From God's Word, the Bible...

But we have this treasure in earthen vessels, that the excellence of the power may be of God and not of us.

2 Corinthians 4:7

Charlie Clapp and the Crooked Stick

Charlie Clapp was well advanced in years when I became his pastor in 1973. He was a devoted Christian who had faithfully served his Lord and his church from his childhood years.

Even though he was very small in stature, Charlie stood tall in our church family. He was known for his wisdom and his sense of humor. The two would often show up together in keen, witty sayings. This one has stayed with me all through the years: "God can hit a mighty good lick with a crooked stick."

God has chosen to advance His work through human instruments. He could work without us, but He has chosen to work through us. That means that God only has crooked sticks with which to hit His licks.

In other words, God doesn't have among His people any perfect instruments. All of His people are flawed in many ways, and all of His people, while forgiven of their sins, will never be completely free from sin in this life.

Take Noah as an example. What a champion for God! Told by the Lord that a great flood was coming, Noah built an ark and preached to his fellow-citizens while he built. But when the floodwaters subsided, Noah left the ark and had an embarrassing episode of drunkenness.

Abraham stands as one of the three towering figures of the Old Testament (along with Moses and David), but Abraham lied about his wife on two occasions.

Isaac struggled with God's determination to set his younger son, Jacob, over the older son, Esau. And Jacob could be conniving and deceitful. Samson got a haircut in the devil's barbershop. Moses lost his temper. Samuel raised sons who were godless. Elijah got so discouraged that he was ready to give up his prophetic ministry. Jeremiah got so fed up with prophesying that he yearned to open an inn in the wilderness (though how he could expect any customers out there is a little uncertain).

I called David one of the three towering figures of the Old Testament. So he was. But David, the man after God's own heart, was guilty of lust, adultery, deceitfulness, and murder in the whole sordid Bathsheba episode.

Things don't get any better in the New Testament era. Zacharias failed to believe a vital message from God. John the Baptist had a bout with doubt, as did Thomas. Simon Peter denied the Lord three times, and, some years later failed to stand for the truth of the gospel at Antioch. John Mark deserted his missionary party.

All of them were crooked sticks, but God used them to hit His licks.

As I read about these and others in the Bible, I can't help but think of Charlie Clapp and the crooked stick.

The truth of Charlie's statement comes home to me, not only when I read the Bible, but also as I read my own life. I am one of God's crooked sticks! Often cold in spirit, careless in thought and in word, wondering about God's ways, fretting about the future, slow to believe—the list, to my shame, could go on.

This I know: if any good has come to anyone from my ministry, the credit and praise must go—not to this crooked stick—but to God. I can say with Charles Spurgeon: "As for myself, I am compelled to say with solemn truthfulness that I am not content with anything that I have ever done...."

While I acknowledge the truth of Charlie's statement, I would add to it one of my own: God can hit a mighty good lick with a straight stick.

In all of human history, there has only been one stick that was truly straight. That is, of course, the Lord Jesus Christ, who never sinned in thought, word or deed. He perfectly complied with the laws of God in every respect. Because He had no sins of His own, He was free to pay for the sins of others. This He did on the cross, there taking the penalty that my sins so deserve.

Yes, Jesus was God's straight stick, and with that stick God hit "a mighty good lick." There's a name for that mighty good lick. It's called redemption. While we thank God for the work He has done with His crooked sticks, we thank Him even more for the work He has done with His straight stick.

-13-

From God's Word, the Bible...

"Although my house is not so with God,
Yet He has made with me an everlasting covenant,
Ordered in all things and secure.
For this is all my salvation and all my desire;
Will He not make it increase?
But the sons of rebellion shall all be as thorns thrust away,
Because they cannot be taken with hands.
But the man who touches them
Must be armed with iron and the shaft of a spear,
And they shall be utterly burned with fire in their place."

2 Samuel 23:5-7

Two Ways to Die

The figure is 55.3 million. That's the number of people who die each year. That's 151,600 each day, 6,316 each hour and 105 each minute.

All people die (with the exception of those who will be living when Jesus comes again—1 Thess. 4:17), but all do not die in the same way.

In his "last words" (2 Sam. 23:1), King David of Israel shows us that there are essentially two ways to die. We can call one the thankful way and the other the thorny way.

David faced death in *the thankful way*. As he saw death coming toward him, he filled his mind with something that robbed death of its terror. This is the thing for which David was thankful. What was it? David himself tells us. It was:

> ... an everlasting covenant,
> Ordered in all things and secure
> (v. 5)

There have been all kinds of covenants or agreements in

human history, but there is only one everlasting covenant. That is God's covenant of grace. This covenant is God's plan of salvation. It is God committing Himself to save His people on the basis of Christ's redeeming work. The Lord Jesus Christ is the mediator in this covenant. He is the One who secures the benefits of it on our behalf, and we participate in it only through faith in Him. To say David was rejoicing in this covenant is to say he was looking forward in faith to the coming of the Lord Jesus.

This covenant is "everlasting." It was contrived in eternity past, and it will continue without end. In its contrivance and continuance it is everlasting.

God has always had only one plan of salvation, and that way is His Son. So we need to rid ourselves of the nonsense that suggests that God tried one plan of salvation, then another, then another, and finally, in desperation, sent His Son.

This covenant is "ordered." Nothing is left to chance in it. There is nothing that is haphazard or slapdash about it. God carefully mapped it all out, and through the centuries He has worked it out just as He planned. God has planned the work and worked the plan.

It is also "secure." Nothing can make it fail. Trust in Christ as your Savior, and nothing—absolutely nothing—can keep you from being saved (Rom. 8:38-39). For God's plan of salvation to fail, God Himself would have to topple from His throne and die! Since God can't die, the plan can't fail.

This covenant was that on which David was pinning his hope. This covenant is, he writes, "all my salvation." David knew his salvation didn't depend partly on God and partly on himself. It was all a matter of God's doing. It was God who would send, it was Jesus who would actually provide salvation for sinners, and it was the Holy Spirit who would apply that salvation to individual sinners.

About God's covenant of grace, David has one more thing to say: "...this is ... all my desire...." Everything David could have ever hoped for was to be found in God's covenant of grace.

How thankful David must have been for that well-ordered and secure covenant as he saw death coming his way! But David couldn't think about the peace that he was enjoying in the face of death without also thinking about the other way of dying—*the thorny way*. He writes:

> *But the sons of rebellion shall*
> *all be as thorns thrust away,*
> *Because they cannot be taken with hands.*
> (v. 6)

Those who reject God's covenant of grace will be thrust away from Him as men thrust away thorns. Men can't pick thorns and brambles up with their hands. So they use long-handled tools. They deal with them from a distance. Those who rebel against God are going to be treated in similar fashion. God is going to stand far away from them as He casts them into eternal destruction.

If we want to tranquilly face death as David did, we must stop rebelling against God, and entrust ourselves completely to God's covenant of grace.

Death is the greatest fact of life. We need a strategy for facing it, and there's really only one effective strategy— God's covenant of grace.

-14-

From God's Word, the Bible...

And beginning at Moses and all the Prophets, He expounded to them in all the Scriptures the things concerning Himself.

Luke 24:27

The Church Search

When we move into a new community, one of our most daunting tasks is finding a church. What are we to look for in a church? One with striking architecture? One with lots of activities? One with thrilling music? One with a pastor who has an entertaining approach to preaching?

I say the church to attend is the one that makes the most of the Lord Jesus. Christianity is about Christ. Take Him out of it, and you no longer have Christianity.

Why should we make much of the Lord Jesus? Why should we magnify Him? There are many reasons. God the Father makes much of Him (Col. 1:19), as does the Holy Spirit (John 16:14). The angels of heaven make much of Him (Heb. 1:6). All of the redeemed of all ages will make much of Him in heaven (Rev. 5:9-10).

On the day of His resurrection, Jesus walked with two of His followers and focused their attention on yet another reason His people are to make much of Him: The Bible makes much of Him!

Think first about the Bible of the Christ.

It should be obvious to us from the words of Jesus that He completely trusted the Scriptures. He doesn't speak to these two disciples along these lines: "You had better be careful about this Bible business. You had better not take it too seriously."

He rather tells them that they had better pay close attention to the Bible. He tells them that the difficulty they were experiencing was because they had been misreading the Bible.

We join them in their error if we read the Bible without looking for the Lord Jesus. He is the subject of it. To miss Him is to misread it.

When Jesus spoke to these men, they only possessed the Old Testament. Jesus accepted the authority of it, and He had already pre-endorsed the authority of the New Testament yet to be written (John 14:26; 16:13).

When the Bible was all done, it was all about Christ. When it was wholly written, it was wholly about Him. In the Old Testament, we have the *anticipation* of Christ. In the gospel accounts we have the *presentation* of Christ, in the epistles we have the *application* of Christ, and in Revelation we have the *culmination* of Christ. But it's all Christ!

That brings us to consider *the Christ of the Bible*, or the Christ that the Bible presents.

I've said that we should go to the church that makes most of Christ. That's true, but not just any Christ will do. It's not enough to merely affirm that the Bible is about Christ. We must see that the Bible presents Him in a particular capacity, that is, as the Savior of His people by virtue of His death on the cross.

It was the cross that those two men walking toward Emmaus couldn't figure out. It didn't fit their notion of the Messiah, but Jesus showed them that the same Scriptures that taught the coming of the Messiah taught the dying of that Messiah (vv. 25-26).

So let us read our Bibles looking for Christ, in the Old Testament as well as in the New Testament. Read the story of Adam, and rejoice in the Lord Jesus who was the second and greater Adam and who succeeded where the first Adam failed.

Think about Abraham leaving that with which he was familiar and comfortable to create a new nation, and rejoice in Jesus leaving the comfort of heaven to create a new people.

Look at the story of Abraham being called to offer Isaac, and rejoice in the fact that God actually did offer His Son.

See in the story of Joseph opening the storehouses of Egypt to feed his starving people a picture of Jesus opening the greater storehouse of heaven to shower spiritual blessings on His people.

Take the story of Job interceding for his stupid friends so that they wouldn't die as a picture of Jesus interceding for us.

Consider the story of Esther being willing to give up her throne for her people as a picture of Jesus actually leaving His heavenly throne.

It's Christ that we need, and if a church refuses to accurately point us to Him, we don't need it.

The words of the Apostle Paul in Ephesians 3:20-21 are so fitting: "Now to Him who is able to do exceedingly abundantly above all that we ask or think, according to the power that works in us, to Him be glory in the church by Christ Jesus to all generations, forever and ever. Amen."

-15-

From God's Word, the Bible...

And the cherubim shall stretch out their wings above, covering the mercy seat with their wings, and they shall face one another; the faces of the cherubim shall be toward the mercy seat. You shall put the mercy seat on top of the ark, and in the ark you shall put the Testimony that I will give you. And there I will meet with you, and I will speak with you from above the mercy seat, from between the two cherubim which are on the ark of the Testimony, about everything which I will give you in commandment to the children of Israel.

From Exodus 25:10-22

An Exact Measurement

Sometimes the gospel shows up when we're not expecting it. Take the Ark of the Covenant for an example. The gospel is truly to be found there.

You probably know about the Ark. It was the most important of all the articles that were first included in the tabernacle and later in the temple that Solomon built. Each of those structures was divided into three parts: an outer court, a holy place, and The Most Holy Place. The latter was the place where only the high priest of Israel could enter. And he could only enter once a year to make atonement for the sins of the people. The Ark was placed in The Most Holy Place.

The Ark had three main parts—a box, a slab, and cherubim.

That box was terrifying. It had in it the Ten Commandments. Those commandments gave solemn testimony to the way God expected people to live and how miserably they failed. It was a box of revelation and condemnation. It revealed God's demands and condemned everybody because no one lived up to God's demands.

Did I say the box *was* terrifying? It *is* terrifying. God hasn't withdrawn or nullified the Ten Commandments. Those commandments express His holy character. To nullify them, He would have to nullify Himself. And those commandments condemn us. Lay your performance alongside any one of the ten, and it will shout "Guilty!" at you.

If the Ark had consisted only of that box, there would be no hope for any of us. But there was also that slab. It sat on top of the box, and it was exactly the same size as the box beneath. That slab, called The Mercy Seat, is where the high priest sprinkled the blood of a sacrifice when he made his annual visit in The Most Holy Place. That sprinkled blood on that slab which exactly covered the box gave a powerful testimony—the blood of the sacrifice was sufficient to cover the demand of that broken law. If The Mercy Seat had been one inch shorter on either side or on both sides, the demands of the box below wouldn't have been covered.

The third main part of the Ark consisted of the cherubim, the highest of the angels. There was one of these angels on each of the end sides of that gold slab, that is, on each side of The Mercy Seat, and each of the two was looking down at it. Because they are associated in Scripture with the throne of God, we should understand the cherubim to represent God Himself. Now we have something very precious, something that takes us to the heart of the atonement. The cherubim, representing God, could not, as it were, see the law and its demands because it was inside the box that was covered by the mercy seat.

Are you thinking that I must be very odd to be interested in a centuries-old relic from the Jewish religion? That old relic points us to the Lord Jesus and His death on the cross!

We might say Jesus went to that cross to be The Mercy Seat for us. God's broken law cries out against each of us: "That person is guilty, and I demand that he or she bear the penalty for violating me."

A fearful penalty it is—eternal separation from God!

What shall we do? How shall we answer the loud shouting of God's broken law? Thank God, there's an answer. The answer is Jesus on the cross. He went there to be our Mercy Seat. He went there to pay the penalty for our law-breaking. On the cross He actually received an eternity's worth of separation from God so that all who believe in Him never have to receive that same penalty themselves.

As the cherubim looked down on The Mercy Seat of old when the atonement was made, so God the Father looked down on the cross when Jesus was there. And when Jesus died, the Father said: "I am satisfied. My Son has borne the penalty demanded by My broken law, and I will not demand it to be paid again by those who believe in Him."

Jesus' death on the cross is the exact measurement for our law breaking. Thank God for Jesus, our Mercy Seat!

The terrors of law and of God
With me can have nothing to do;
My Savior's obedience and blood
Hide all my transgressions from view.
(Augustus Toplady)

-16-

From God's Word, the Bible...

Then Elisha said, "Shoot"; and he shot. And he said, "The arrow of the LORD's deliverance and the arrow of deliverance from Syria; for you must strike the Syrians at Aphek till you have destroyed them." Then he said, "Take the arrows"; so he took them. And he said to the king of Israel, "Strike the ground"; so he struck three times, and stopped. And the man of God was angry with him, and said, "You should have struck five or six times; then you would have struck Syria till you had destroyed it! But now you will strike Syria only three times."

But it is good to be zealous in a good thing always, and not only when I am present with you.

From 2 Kings 13:14-19; Galatians 4:18

Zeal in Religion

Here we have the story of a king visiting a dying prophet. This happened so long ago—thousands of years—that we might conclude that it has no value for us. We would be wrong to think so. This story puts before each of us this probing question: How much zeal do we have for a good cause? Or we can put it in this way: Are we satisfied with doing little for a cause that calls for us to do much?

Think about *the good cause*. Joash was a man in great trouble when he came to the prophet Elisha. The Syrian army had already captured some of the cities of Israel and were menacing more. It looked as if the whole nation might very well be destroyed. The good cause placed before Joash was the preservation of his kingdom.

It's interesting that Joash, an idolater, turned to the prophet in the midst of his despair. His visit to Elisha may indicate that he was beginning to realize that his idolatry wasn't working out so well.

A second truth for us to consider is *the promise of victory*.

The prophet had an answer for the king. Because he,

Elisha, embodied or represented God's Word, we can say that the Word of God had an answer for Joash. God's Word still has answers for our deepest dilemmas and our most profound perplexities.

The dying prophet told the king to take a bow and some arrows. He then told him to put his hand on the bow. When this was done, Elisha put his hands on the king's hands. Next he told the king to shoot an arrow. As the arrow went flying through the air, Elisha cried: "The arrow of the LORD's deliverance and the arrow of deliverance from Syria" (v. 17).

After the one arrow was shot, Elisha commanded Joash to strike the ground with the other arrows.

What did it all mean? The hands of the prophet represented God's hand. The arrows represented victory. The prophet was promising that God would give Joash victory over the Syrians.

That leads us to *the tragic failure*.

Here is the crucial thing—victory would come only as Joash himself desired it and was zealous for it. So the striking of the remaining arrows on the ground was a test, and Joash failed the test. He struck the ground only three times. If he had struck it five or six times, his victory over Syria would be complete. But having struck it only three times, his victory would be partial.

The difference between total victory and partial victory lay in the heart of Joash himself. A totally zealous heart would lead to total victory, but a partially zealous heart would only lead to partial victory.

By the way, the prophecy of Elisha came true. Joash went on to defeat the Syrians, but only three times (v. 25).

We who know the Lord should let this episode speak powerfully to us. Do we believe that we are engaged in a good cause, the Lord's cause? Do we understand that the Lord has appointed certain ways for His cause to prosper—

prayer, faithfully supporting the preaching and teaching of God's Word, fervently protecting the unity of the church, generously giving our money to advance the church? Are we diligently and zealously doing these things? Or are we, like Joash, only halfhearted? If they were pressed on the matter, many these days would have to say that they don't have much zeal for the Lord's cause. They're content to do very little when they could and should be doing much.

We would do well to let Joash drive us to Jesus. How thankful we should be that Jesus wasn't like Joash. The Lord Jesus was totally devoted to His cause—providing salvation for sinners—and He didn't allow anything to deter Him. He didn't stop short of reaching His goal. When He cried out from the cross, "It is finished!" (John 19:30), He was announcing that He hadn't failed in doing the good thing He came to do. His complete victory for sinners means salvation for all of them who will repent of their sins and trust in Him.

-17-

From God's Word, the Bible...

Now it came to pass, as He sat at the table with them, that He took bread, blessed and broke it, and gave it to them. Then their eyes were opened and they knew Him; and He vanished from their sight. And they said to one another, "Did not our heart burn within us while He talked with us on the road, and while He opened the Scriptures to us?" So they rose up that very hour and returned to Jerusalem, and found the eleven and those who were with them gathered together, saying, "The Lord is risen indeed, and has appeared to Simon!" And they told about the things that had happened on the road, and how He was known to them in the breaking of bread.

From Luke 24:28-35

Gospel Feeling

In Romans 6:17, the Apostle Paul writes: "…you obeyed from the heart that form of doctrine to which you were delivered."

This verse shows us how God intends for us to function. We are to receive the truth of God with our minds. Because that truth is by nature inexpressibly glorious, we are to be moved by it. Then on the basis of what we have understood with our minds and felt with our hearts, we are to take action.

True religion involves both our minds and our feelings. Some forget about the former and stress the latter. They emphasize feeling too much. These come to church for one reason. They want to have an emotional experience. They're not interested in applying their minds to the truth of God with a view to mastering it. What matters to them is getting whipped into an emotional frenzy. If these people had been present on Mt. Carmel with Elijah and the prophets of Baal, they would have sided with the latter. Why? The prophets of Baal had all the emotion. But let's never forget that they didn't have the truth. And God places a premium on truth. He tells us to buy the truth and not sell it (Prov. 23:23).

The other extreme is to not emphasize feeling at all and to not feel anything. Those in this category are content to have nothing but the truth delivered. They are suspicious of anyone who is touched or moved. These people need to take to heart the words of Jonathan Edwards: "True religion, in great part, consists in holy affections."

True religion has been contrived by God in such a way that it ought to thrill our souls. But many Christians would have to admit that it has been a very long time since they felt any thrill in connection with their Christianity.

Luke tells us about two men who walked with Jesus on the day of His resurrection. These men experienced the thrilling nature of true religion. Their own testimony is that their hearts burned within them (Luke 24:32).

It's easy for us to so misread this passage that we find ourselves speaking along these lines: "If the Lord Jesus were to appear and walk with me, my heart would burn, too."

If we find ourselves saying that, we are missing this vital point: the hearts of these two men burned within them before they knew that it was the risen Christ with whom they were walking.

They themselves tell us that their hearts burned within them while they were on the road with Him. They didn't know it was Jesus that they were walking with until after the journey was complete and they sat down to have supper with Him (vv. 28-32).

If they didn't know they were walking with the risen Christ, what made their hearts burn during that time? Let them answer. It was "while He opened the Scriptures" (v. 32). More specifically, their hearts burned as He showed them that the crucifixion that perplexed them (vv. 18-21) and the resurrection that puzzled them (vv. 22-24) were both required by the Old Testament Scriptures.

You and I have even more of the Scriptures than those men possessed. If their hearts burned within them as they realized the truth of their Scriptures, should not our hearts burn within us as we read and study the Bible? We shouldn't study the Bible merely to accumulate facts. We're intended to feel something as we read about our Savior coming from the glory of heaven to live in complete obedience to God, to die as our substitute, and to spring from the grave in glorious, resurrection life.

If these truths don't make our hearts burn, we may be sure that it's because we are "slow of heart" (v. 26). It's not that we don't have the truth. It's not that the truth isn't unspeakably glorious. It's rather that we're slow to believe it and apply it. It's to our shame that our hearts can be so quick to embrace the passing things of this world and so slow to embrace the things of God. Our need is to know the truth and to feel the truth.

If we don't feel anything, do we have anything? May these thoughts drive us to a renewed commitment to seeking the Lord in His Word and to find our hearts warmed with a holy zeal for Him as we endeavor to live in light of the grace of the gospel.

-18-

From God's Word, the Bible...

Then he said to them, "Go your way, eat the fat, drink the sweet, and send portions to those for whom nothing is prepared; for this day is holy to our Lord. Do not sorrow, for the joy of the LORD is your strength."

Nehemiah 8:10

Strength from the Joy of the LORD

"Do not sorrow, for the joy of the LORD is your strength." That's what Nehemiah said to the people of Israel. Ezra the priest had just preached to them (v. 8), and they, devastated by the realization of their failure to obey God, began to weep and mourn. As the weeping continued, Nehemiah offered these words to console and comfort them.

These words have always seemed backwards to me. If I had been there, I would have expected Nehemiah to say: "The strength of the Lord is your joy."

That makes sense, doesn't it? Don't you rejoice in knowing that the Lord is unlimited in power? Of course you do.

But that's not what Nehemiah said. He said: "the joy of the LORD is your strength." Nehemiah isn't telling us that joy comes our way from realizing the Lord is strong. He is telling us that strength comes our way from realizing the Lord is joyful.

What we have in this verse, then, are words for all who find themselves in need of strength. That includes all of us. We find the life business to be very challenging. Its demands seem to be too demanding, and its difficulties seem to be too difficult. Life has a way of depleting our strength even while it calls us to be strong.

If we feel that life has overmatched and overpowered us, we would do well to give Nehemiah's principle a try. Here it is again: There is strength in knowing that the Lord Himself is joyful.

All too frequently we Christians allow ourselves to have the impression that God is always angry with us. We know God is just, and His justice doesn't allow Him to take our sins lightly. Moreover, we have a tendency to think that God's justice wipes out His joy. But every attribute of God is always fully and perfectly expressed in God. Therefore, even while His justice is in full force, it doesn't destroy His joy. In His justice, He is joyful. In His joy, He is just.

Nowhere does the Bible tell us that God takes our sins lightly, but neither does it tell us that our sins destroy His joy (Job 35:6-8).

What causes God to be joyful at all times? Why is He always happy? For one thing, He takes joy in Himself. As God, he is perfect in every respect. If He didn't delight in His own perfection, He wouldn't be perfect. It would be impossible for God to be perfect if He didn't find joy in His perfection.

God also delights in His Son and in the redeeming work of His Son. He also finds delight in His creation. And, yes, He delights in His people even though they are far from perfect. He delights in their growth, as small as it is; in their prayers, as feeble as they are (Prov. 15:8); and in their service, as poor as it is. He ever finds joy in forgiving His people when they come to Him in true confession.

How does the joy of the Lord provide strength for us? It gives us strength for worship. It would be very difficult to worship an unhappy, miserable God. It gives us strength for service. It would be very hard to serve an unhappy God who can never be pleased. It gives us strength for prayer. We would find it impossible to pray to a God who is never happy with us or with our prayers. It gives us strength to witness. It would be very difficult to tell others about an unhappy God. It gives us strength to die because death for Christians means coming into the presence of their happy God.

Jesus is our example on this issue, even as He is on every other issue. The cost of redemption for sinners was so great that we might be inclined to think there couldn't possibly be any joy in it. If that's our view, we're wrong. He found strength to do the work of redemption because He kept His eye fixed on the joy of what He was doing. There was strength for the doing of it because there was joy in the doing of it.

Do you find your strength in the Lord and in His many wonderful attributes?

-19-

From God's Word, the Bible...

If you then, being evil, know how to give good gifts to your children, how much more will your heavenly Father give the Holy Spirit to those who ask Him!

Luke 11:13

Praying for the Holy Spirit

Jesus promises that His Father will "give the Holy Spirit to those who ask Him."

Why should we be praying for the Holy Spirit? The first reason is because *the Lord expects us to do so*. Jesus wouldn't have mentioned the Father's willingness to bestow the Spirit if He didn't expect us to be praying for the Spirit.

Some say that these words from Jesus carried with them an expiration date, that is, Jesus was only telling His followers to pray for the Holy Spirit until the Day of Pentecost. They maintain that this prayer was fully answered when the Holy Spirit fell on believers that day, and there is now no need to continue praying for Him. In their estimation, to pray for the Holy Spirit is like praying for Jesus to come again as a baby in Bethlehem.

But Jesus didn't indicate any expiration date when He told His disciples to pray for the Spirit. This petition is open-ended. As far as I'm concerned, I would rather pray for the

Spirit and finally learn that it wasn't necessary than to not pray for Him and finally learn that it was vitally necessary.

A second reason for praying for the Spirit is this: *People can't be saved without the power of the Holy Spirit.*

The church is to be confronting men and women with the reality of their sins and to be pointing them to the Lord Jesus Christ as the only way for them to be forgiven of their sins and delivered from judgment to come.

We can't convince a single person of a single sin without the power of the Spirit, and we can't convince a single person to receive Christ without that same power. The Spirit is the One who convicts sinners. He is the One who convinces people of judgment to come, and He is the One who convinces sinners that the Lord Jesus is the Savior (John 16:7-11).

If salvation is bound up in the work of the Holy Spirit, we must be asking for the Holy Spirit.

Here's a third reason for us to be praying for the Holy Spirit—*He must surely be grieved by much of what is going on in the church today.*

It's true that the Holy Spirit came upon the church at Pentecost, and He has never left. But we should think about the different ways one can be present—in a smiling, warm way or in a cool, withdrawn way. I'm suggesting that while the Spirit is still present, He isn't smiling on the church today. He is, as it were, in the room, but He is standing in the corner with His face turned away. He is present, but He is grieved. Yes, the Holy Spirit can be grieved (Eph. 4:30) and quenched (1 Thess. 4:19). He is grieved by:

- our dependence on slick promotions, clever personalities, and entertaining programs;
- our watering down of the message of the Bible so we don't offend people;
- our casual treatment of His day and His house;

- the pettiness and childishness that leads to bickering and quarreling and that destroys the unity of the church;
- our love of pleasure and our own comfort;
- our lack of concern for the unsaved;
- our lack of holiness in thought, word, and deed;
- and, yes, He is grieved by our failure to pray for Him!

Let's also add yet another reason we should be praying for the Spirit, namely, *the Father's willingness to answer that prayer*.

Jesus assures us of this, and His assurance should be enough for us. Moreover, we can leaf through the pages of church history and find instances of God's people praying for the Spirit and receiving the Spirit.

In his remarkable book *The Forgotten Spurgeon*, Iain H. Murray notes that Spurgeon came to London "conscious that God had been hiding His face from His people." So Spurgeon said to his church:

> All we want is the Spirit of God. Dear Christian friends, go home and pray for it; give yourselves no rest till God reveals Himself; do not tarry where you are, do not be content to go on in your everlasting jogtrot as you have done; do not be content with the mere round of formalities. Awake, O Zion; awake, awake, awake![2]

---

[2] Iain H. Murray, *The Forgotten Spurgeon* Banner of Truth Trust, Edinburgh, (Second Edition), 1978, p. 34-5

-20-

From God's Word, the Bible...

I would have lost heart, unless I had believed
That I would see the goodness of the LORD
In the land of the living.

Psalm 27:13

God's Goodness in Revival

The psalmist is talking our language in the first part of this verse. He's talking about losing heart. This is what many of God's people are experiencing in these days. What does it mean to lose heart? It means to be discouraged or despondent.

It's very easy to understand why discouragement is so prevalent among Christians. Our society continues to plummet into greater depths of evil. Christianity continues to lose its grip on the thinking of most people. And many pastors and churches appear to have lost their grip on their basic task—preaching the gospel of Christ. Many would be hard-pressed to give a clear explanation of the very message they're supposed to be proclaiming.

The psalmist can help all who find themselves in the grip of discouragement. He tells us that he had just about lost heart. What brought him to this point? He was surrounded by people who hated him and what he stood for, just as

Christians are today.

But then something happened, something that caused his discouragement to melt away. He got to thinking about the goodness of the Lord and how the people of God had experienced it so many times down through the centuries. Then it hit him! The goodness of the Lord hadn't perished! It was still operative and available. It wasn't just a thing of the past. As he reflected on it, the psalmist realized that he could see that same goodness "in the land of the living," that is, in the here and now.

Do we believe as the psalmist did? Do we believe that we can see the goodness of the Lord here and now?

What does it mean to see the goodness of the Lord? It means that God makes His goodness visible in a very clear and undisputable way.

The goodness of God is ever present. You and I couldn't draw our next breath were it not for His goodness. Much to our shame, we get so used to God's goodness that we start taking it for granted, so much so that we don't even realize that we're receiving it.

While God's goodness is always with us, there are special seasons of His goodness. A revival is a special season of God's goodness. What is a revival? It's God moving in a powerful way upon His people to restore them to spiritual vitality and health. Revival is not a meeting. It's a movement—a movement of God.

Some think that we are wrong to look for such a season in this time. They think revival is impossible. Some rule it out on prophetic grounds. I've heard many preachers speak in this way: "The next item on God's agenda is not a revival, but the rapture."

This view makes it seem as if we are to accept the apathy and indifference that abounds in the church today. It seems to me that the Bible never uses prophetic teaching to encourage apathy about spiritual matters. Quite the opposite is the case (2 Peter 3:10-13). If the Bible doesn't use prophecy to excuse apathy, should we?

Others rule out any possibility of revival on sociological or cultural grounds. They tell us that revival was a phenomenon that occurred in a less complicated time, and that time has forever passed. Yes, society has changed—and how!—but has God changed?

Yet other people dismiss the possibility of revival on practical grounds, telling us that evil is too strongly entrenched for revival to occur. But a quick reading of church history tells us that God has shown the goodness of revival in other times of horrendous evil. Is anything too hard for the Lord? (See Gen. 18:14.)

The question that ought to concern us is not whether God desires to send revival. The question is rather whether we desire for God to send it. We are always inclined to concern ourselves with God's business instead of with our own. Our business, no matter how evil the times are and no matter how near the end we may be, is to earnestly desire God's good work of revival and to seek it through real repentance and fervent prayer.

-21-

From God's Word, the Bible...

See then that you walk circumspectly, not as fools but as wise, redeeming the time, because the days are evil.
Therefore do not be unwise, but understand what the will of the Lord is. And do not be drunk with wine, in which is dissipation; but be filled with the Spirit, speaking to one another in psalms and hymns and spiritual songs, singing and making melody in your heart to the Lord, giving thanks always for all things to God the Father in the name of our Lord Jesus Christ, submitting to one another in the fear of God.

Ephesians 5:15-21

Wise Up, O Men of God

The parents along with their young son were in their usual places for worship on a Sunday morning. The first hymn was announced. It was William Pierson Merrill's hymn *Rise Up, O Men of God*. As the singing went along, the parents could tell that their little boy was replacing "rise up" with "wise up."

It wasn't a bad substitution. God's men, and women, need to "wise up" as well as "rise up."

The Apostle Paul definitely wanted his readers in Ephesus to "wise up" about their walk in this world. He tells them to walk "circumspectly." That means they were to walk carefully. They were to understand that the world is not a friend to the children of God. It rather presents them with many dangers. So they must pick their way carefully as they walk in it. The unbeliever is infatuated with the world. He loves everything about it, but the Christian sees through the world. He doesn't deny that there are good things in this world to be enjoyed, but he also sees the evil of the world.

How do we walk wisely in this world? *First, by using our time wisely* (v.16). Christians shouldn't be content to just spend time or "kill" time. They see their time as a stewardship that is to be used for the honor of their Master, the Lord Jesus.

One incentive for using our time wisely is, Paul says, that "the days are evil."

Evil days obviously give us plenty of opportunities to do evil, but they also give us plenty of opportunities to do good. We should always be on the lookout for the opportunities presented to us by this evil world—opportunities to do good—and in doing so, show the difference God has made in our lives.

We would all do well to do a time inventory. Are we using our time wisely? Are we using our time on the Lord's Day to be in His house? Are we using our time at home to live in a godly manner, speaking words of grace and acting in a Christlike way? Are we using our time at work to show that Christians think, speak, and act on a higher level?

Walking wisely in this world is also a matter of *understanding the will of the Lord* (v. 17).

People of the world can concern themselves with these questions: What will bring me more comfort? What will make me more money? What will bring me more pleasure? What will make me more popular?

But the Christian is called to constantly ask himself this question: What does the Lord want me to do in this situation? When he asks that, he doesn't look for guidance written in the clouds. He looks for the guidance written in God's Word. God primarily guides His people through His Word, and the more Word-centered we are, the more guidance we will find.

And walking wisely in this world means *being "filled with the Spirit"* (v. 18).

We are all filled with something, and it is usually impossible to be around someone for very long without becoming aware of his or her filling. One may be filled with his career, another with sports, still yet another with computers. This man here may be consumed with his car, and the lady over there with travel.

Paul tells us to be filled with the Spirit. It's important to note that he contrasts this with drunkenness. He writes: "And do not be drunk with wine, in which is dissipation; but be filled with the Spirit."

When a person is drunk, his or her thinking, speaking, and walking are all affected. By using this contrast, Paul is telling us to let the Spirit of God control our thinking, our speaking, and our walking, that is, the totality of our conduct.

Since the Spirit of God is the Spirit of praise, we will, if we are Spirit-filled, be people who praise God (v. 19).

And since the Spirit of God is the Spirit of Christ, if we are Spirit-filled, we will be thanking God for the Lord Jesus (v. 20) and will be submitting ourselves to Him (v. 21).

Was the little boy right to sing "Wise up, O men of God"? No, not technically. But, then again, maybe he was on to something.

-22-

From God's Word, the Bible...

And Joseph said to his brethren, "I am dying; but God will surely visit you, and bring you out of this land to the land of which He swore to Abraham, to Isaac, and to Jacob." Then Joseph took an oath from the children of Israel, saying, "God will surely visit you, and you shall carry up my bones from here."

Genesis 50:24-25

Bones in the Bible (1)

In my estimation, there are three unusual stories about bones in the Old Testament. The first has to do with Joseph, the second with Elisha, and the last with Ezekiel. Each of these three accounts has a message of importance for us.

The bones of Joseph speak to us about faith in God's promises. We could call it faith in God's faithfulness.

You remember the story of Joseph. Sold into slavery by his jealous brothers, he rose by the hand of the sovereign God to a position of great prominence in Egypt, second only to Pharaoh himself. Joseph used his position to save his people, the Israelites, from a horrible famine by bringing them out of the land of Canaan and resettling them in Egypt.

Joseph spent his entire adult life—which lasted a long time—in Egypt. He knew his people would be there a long time as well, but he also knew that Egypt wouldn't be the final home for them. Joseph knew this because of the promise God had given to his great-grandfather Abraham (Gen. 13:12,14-17; 15:18-21; 17:8), his grandfather Isaac (Gen. 26:3-

5), and his father Jacob (Gen. 35:12). The same God who promised the land of Canaan to Joseph's people also promised that they would be enslaved in a foreign land for four hundred years after which God would bring them back to Canaan (Gen. 17:13-16).

When the time came for Joseph to die, those promises were much on his mind. Being fully aware of God's faithfulness to His promises, Joseph knew full well that his people would eventually be released from slavery in Egypt and would once again dwell in Canaan. Although he spent so much of his life in Egypt, Joseph wanted his bones to be ultimately buried in Canaan. All through those years in Egypt, Joseph's heart had been in Canaan.

It all turned out just as Joseph expected. God used Moses to deliver the Israelites from Egypt and Joshua to resettle them in Canaan. And, yes, when the Israelites left Egypt, they took the bones of Joseph along with them (Exod. 13:19).

So Joseph was a man of faith (Heb. 11:22). What is faith? Many think it's a matter of psyching ourselves up to believe whatever we want to be true will be true. They equate faith with optimism or positive thinking. But, no, that isn't faith. Faith is believing the Word of God. Where there is no word from God, there can be no faith (Rom. 10:17). On the other hand, when we do have a word from God, we can have certainty because God never fails to keep a promise (Josh. 21:45; 23:14; 1 Kings 8:56).

The question before us isn't whether God has made glorious promises regarding His people. He has. The question is rather whether we believe in those promises to the degree that we should. Charles Spurgeon used to say: "Brethren, be great believers. Little faith will take your souls to heaven. But great faith will bring heaven to your souls."

Heaven is recording the history of God's people in every era. How fascinating it will be to read heaven's history!

What will it say about our era? Will we be noted as a people of big faith or little faith?

One of the wonderful promises God has given us pertains to our bones. The Lord tells us that death is not the final word for God's people. Those who die will be raised from their graves when Jesus comes again (1 Thess. 4:16). That promise is most certainly a "sting-remover" when we face death.

By the way, that promise also pertains to Joseph, even though his bones have long since turned to dust. Dust is no problem for the Lord! He will call Joseph's body from that dust and change it into a glorious body over which death will have no power (Phil. 3:20-21).

Let's make sure we never forget that glorious resurrection life is a privilege the Lord Jesus Christ purchased for His people by the shedding of His blood on the cross. So while we praise Joseph as an example of faith, we reserve our greater praise for Jesus, the object of our faith.

> *Mine eyes shall see Him in that day,*
> *The God that died for me,*
> *And all my rising bones shall say,*
> *"Lord, who is like to Thee?"*

-23-

From God's Word, the Bible...

Then Elisha died, and they buried him. And the raiding bands from Moab invaded the land in the spring of the year. So it was, as they were burying a man, that suddenly they spied a band of raiders; and they put the man in the tomb of Elisha; and when the man was let down and touched the bones of Elisha, he revived and stood on his feet.

2 Kings 13:20-21

Bones in the Bible (2)

We are in the middle of what we might call "The Bone Trilogy," that is, three stories of the Old Testament that have to do with bones. We are looking at them because each proclaims to us a message of importance.

The bones of Joseph set before us the faithfulness of God. God had made certain promises regarding the people of Israel, and Joseph believed those promises.

The bones of Elisha have a different message to convey. They tell us to believe in the power of God. God has such power that He can overcome seemingly impossible situations.

Elisha had only been dead a few months when Moabite raiders began invading the land of Israel. Some Israelites were in the process of burying a dead man when they saw a band of those raiders. What happened next is a bit unclear. It seems that they were in the process of preparing a grave for this man when they spotted the raiders and abandoned their preparations in favor of putting him in the nearby tomb of Elisha. This much is clear: in their haste, they allowed the body of the dead man to touch the bones of the prophet. That led to an indescribably amazing thing: coming into contact with the bones of Elisha caused that dead man to come back to life!

Can you imagine the shock of the ones doing the burying? It's a wonder that they didn't trade places with the dead man. Seeing him alive was so shocking that they themselves could have died from fright, but they were evidently able to absorb the shock enough to keep breathing.

No one should come away from this passage saying, "I surely wish I had one of Elisha's bones. Just think of what I could do with it!"

This account isn't here to tell us that there was power in the bones of Elisha but rather to tell us that there is power in the God of Elisha. It was God who used Elisha's bones on this occasion. Leave God out of the equation, and Elisha's bones would have been no different than those of anyone else. Without God, ten thousand dead men—or a hundred thousand—could touch the bones of Elisha and still be dead.

But God is here although He isn't mentioned by name, and He is here in astounding power. Many immediately dismiss this miracle. They say that they have "a problem" with this account. I agree. Those who reject the miracles of the Bible do have a problem, but their problem is not what they think. It's not so much the miracles as it is the truth that the miracles are designed to convey, namely, this is God's world and He can step into it at any time to drive truth home to our hearts that we might otherwise miss.

We need to make up our minds about this question: Is God unlimited in power or not? If we admit that His power is unlimited, why do we insist on trying to limit it? Why do we want to believe that God's power can accomplish this over here and not that over there? If we assume that God's power wasn't sufficient for Him to do this miracle—raising this man from the dead—don't we have to rule out every miracle of the Bible? If we rule all of them out, we must rule out the resurrection of Jesus Himself, and if we rule that out, we must give up all hope of Him being our Savior.

Christianity, by its very nature, is supernatural. Take out the supernatural, and you no longer have Christianity and all the benefits it offers.

This miracle occurred at an exceedingly dark point in the life of the nation of Israel. Wickedness was abounding on every hand (vv. 3,6,11), and Elisha was dead. By performing this miracle, God showed that although Elisha was dead, He, God, wasn't dead, and the nation itself could be delivered from death by staying in contact with the Word of God that Elisha so capably represented.

The dead man in this story was resurrected so he could resume life as he had known it before and to eventually die again. But something even more marvelous awaits all who trust in Christ—entering into glorious resurrection life never to die again.

Have you come to know the wonderful new life that God gives to all who trust in Christ alone for salvation? In the Gospel of John, these words of Christ are recorded: "I am the resurrection and the life. He who believes in Me, though he may die, he shall live. And whoever lives and believes in Me shall never die" (John 11:25, 26).

-24-

From God's Word, the Bible...

Then He said to me, "Son of man, these bones are the whole house of Israel. They indeed say, 'Our bones are dry, our hope is lost, and we ourselves are cut off!' Therefore prophesy and say to them, 'Thus says the Lord GOD: "Behold, O My people, I will open your graves and cause you to come up from your graves, and bring you into the land of Israel. Then you shall know that I am the LORD, when I have opened your graves, O My people, and brought you up from your graves."'"

Ezekiel 37:11-13

Bones in the Bible (3)

Now we come to the bones of Ezekiel. This time the bones are not his. They are rather the many, many bones that he saw in a vision.

Ezekiel was the prophet with a very unusual ministry. He was one of the Jews that had been taken into captivity by the Babylonians, and he was called by God to serve as a prophet to his fellow-captives there in Babylon.

What a daunting task! The Jewish captives were in deep, dark despondency. God had promised that the captivity wouldn't be the final word for them. They would eventually be restored to their homeland. But while the captives knew about that promise, they probably often found it hard to believe. Babylon was so strong, and they, the Jewish people, were so weak! What chance was there of the promise being fulfilled, they might have wondered.

Then the day came when the Lord gave Ezekiel a most encouraging vision. He showed him a valley of bones. These bones were great in number and very dry.

The Lord had a question for Ezekiel: "Son of man, can

these bones live?" (v. 3).

Ezekiel knew this—when the Lord asks a question, it's not because He doesn't know the answer. So Ezekiel gave a very astute answer: "O Lord GOD, you know" (v. 3).

Then the Lord told Ezekiel to prophesy to the bones, and the bones began to join together, and sinew, flesh, and skin covered them. So Ezekiel had gone from a valley of bones to a valley of corpses. But the Lord told him to prophesy again. As he did so, breath entered those corpses, and they "stood upon their feet, an exceedingly great army" (v. 10).

The Lord left no doubt about the meaning of the vision. Those dry bones represented the Jewish people there in Babylon. Their future as a nation seemed about as impossible and hopeless as those bones being turned into a mighty army. But in the vision God did exactly that. He turned bones into human beings. He did the seemingly impossible, and He used that vision to pledge that He would do the seemingly impossible with the Jews. He would bring them out of captivity and restore them to their homeland (vv. 11-14).

God would do this because He had promised to do it and because He had the power to do it. His message to those captives amounted to this: Don't look at your circumstances; look at your God.

By the way, God did exactly as He promised. The Persians conquered Babylon, and God put it in the heart of the Persian king, Cyrus, to send the Jews back home. It was God faithfully keeping His promise by exerting His power.

So while the bones of Joseph speak about God's faithfulness, and the bones of Elisha about His power, the bones that Ezekiel saw speak of both.

There have been many times in which it appeared as if God either would not or could not keep His promises. Giving aged Abraham and Sarah a son, delivering the Israelites from their bondage in Egypt and settling them in the land of Canaan, and using various judges to defeat seemingly invincible enemies are all examples of God moving in power to do what He had promised to do.

It must have often looked as if God had either forgotten His promise to send the Messiah or as if He lacked the power to actually do it. But in His own time, God kept that promise and Jesus, the Messiah, came to provide salvation for sinners. Now God has promised that this same Jesus will come again to take His people to Himself and to usher them into eternal glory. Many doubt that this promise will be fulfilled, but we who know the Lord simply look back to those other times in which God's promises seemed to fail only to gloriously succeed. We look at those times and remind ourselves of God's faithfulness and power. When it comes to a promise from God we look to the bones of Joseph, Elisha, and Ezekiel and join Charles Wesley in saying:

> *Faith, mighty faith, the promise sees,*
> *And looks to God alone;*
> *Laughs at impossibilities,*
> *And cries, "It shall be done."*

-25-

From God's Word, the Bible...

All that the Father gives Me will come to Me, and the one who comes to Me I will by no means cast out.

John 6:37

A Doctor's Surprise

A medical doctor was so impressed with an anonymously published hymn that he carried it with him. His calls took him one day to a patient whose constant physical illness had brought deep depression upon her.

Thinking she might be cheered by the words of the hymn he carried, the doctor pulled it out of his pocket and read it.

After reading the hymn, the doctor was surprised to hear his patient say that she was very familiar with it because she had written it. Her name? Charlotte Elliott.

Charlotte spent the first several years of her life resenting God. Angry with Him because of her poor health, she said: "If God loved me, He wouldn't have treated me this way."

Her family's concern for her led them to invite the well-known Swiss evangelist, César Malan, to take a meal with them. The date was May 9, 1822. Their hope that Malan would be able to help Charlotte appeared to be dashed when she flew into a rant against God and her family. Profoundly embarrassed, her family withdrew, leaving Charlotte and Malan alone at the table.

He gently suggested to her that the only way for her to have peace was by embracing the very faith she so utterly detested. "If I should want to become a Christian, what would I have to do?" Charlotte asked. Malan responded by telling her that she must come to God just as she was. "Just as I am?" she asked. "Come just as you are," he said.

Malan stayed in touch with Charlotte after that visit, constantly urging her to look to the cross of Christ for salvation. At last she did, coming to faith when she was thirty-two years of age.

A few years after her conversion, she began to feel so useless and discouraged that she even doubted her salvation. She recalled the words of Cesar Malan: "Come just as you are." Taking up her pen, she wrote:

> *Just as I am without one plea,*
> *But that Thy blood was shed for me,*
> *And that Thou bidd'st me come to Thee –*
> *O Lamb of God, I come, I come!*

> *Just as I am and waiting not*
> *To rid my soul of one dark blot;*
> *To Thee whose blood can cleanse each spot,*
> *O Lamb of God, I come, I come!*

> *Just as I am, though tossed about*
> *With many a conflict, many a doubt,*
> *Fightings and fears within, without—*
> *O Lamb of God, I come, I come!*

> *Just as I am, Thou wilt receive,*
> *Wilt welcome, pardon, cleanse, relieve.*
> *Because Thy promise I believe,*
> *O Lamb of God, I come, I come!*

The fact that her doctor found Charlotte in such a low state after she wrote this hymn reminds us that coming to faith in Christ doesn't mean all our problems vanish. Our "fightings and fears" come from Satan. Before we're saved, he fights to keep us from Christ, and he tries to make us fear that God won't forgive us. After we're saved, he fights to keep us from enjoying and serving Christ, and he tries to make us fear that we have never come to Christ at all.

Coming to Christ solves our biggest problem. It acquits us of our law-breaking and gives us right standing with God, but it also brings us into a whole new set of difficulties. The Christian life is not a picnic; it is a war (Eph. 6:10-20). Charlotte learned this very well, and expressed it in another hymn:

Christian, seek not yet repose, Hear thy gracious Savior say;
Thou art in the midst of foes: Watch and pray.

Principalities and powers, Mustering their unseen array,
Wait for thy unguarded hours: Watch and pray.

Gird thy heavenly armor on, Wear it every night and day;
Ambushed lies the evil one: Watch and pray.

Charlotte Elliott had her struggles as a Christian, but she learned to "watch and pray," and, according to one of her friends, she enjoyed more and more peace as the years passed by. At age eighty-two, she died and entered into perfect peace because of Jesus who saves sinners that come to Him just as they are. When Charlotte met her doctor in heaven's glory, I think she might have said: "Do you remember how I was when you read my hymn to me? Just look at me now."

-26-

From God's Word, the Bible...

Then she named the child Ichabod, saying, "The glory has departed from Israel!" because the ark of God had been captured and because of her father-in-law and her husband. And she said, "The glory has departed from Israel, for the ark of God has been captured."

1 Samuel 4:21-22

Goodbye to Glory

What sad and sorrowful days for Israel! It was bad enough that they were soundly defeated in battle by their archenemies, the Philistines. But there was more. The Philistines had also made off with the Ark of the Covenant.

The Ark should never have been on the battlefield in the first place. But after an initial defeat at the hands of the Philistines, the elders of Israel thought bringing the Ark to the battlefield would ensure victory. How wrong they were! It was not the Ark of God that could give them victory; it was rather the God of the Ark. Yes, God had promised that Israel would triumph over her enemies if they would live in faithful obedience to His commandments. Ah, there was the rub. The Israelites and their leaders had strayed far from God. They were trampling upon His commandments with an alarming disregard. The day of reckoning had come. So when the Ark of God went into battle, God didn't go with the Ark. And Israel was even more decisively defeated.

Two of Israel's leaders in this debacle were the priests Hophni and Phinehas. First-class scoundrels these two! They stood front and center in the wicked living that was so prevalent in those days (1 Sam. 2:12-17). And they finally paid the price for their godlessness as they died in battle.

Phinehas' wife immediately went into labor when she heard the news of her husband's death, but, tragically, as the child was born she died. And with her dying breath, she named her son "Ichabod" and said: "The glory has departed from Israel." The name "Ichabod" means "inglorious."

She was right to say the glory had departed from Israel, but she was wrong if she thought that it had happened on that day. It had happened long before when the leaders and the people began to turn their backs on God. The glory didn't depart because Israel was defeated and the Ark was captured. Israel was defeated and the Ark was captured because the glory had already departed. The departed Ark was not the cause of departed glory. It was the result of it.

If we think this ancient story has nothing to do with us, we are as mistaken as the elders of Israel when they went charging into battle with the Ark. The sad truth is "Ichabod" could be scrawled across the doors of many churches, the pulpits in those churches, and the individual lives of many church members.

The glory of the church is in what the Apostle Paul calls "the glorious gospel of the blessed God" (1 Tim. 1:11). The gospel is the good news of what God has done in and through His Son Jesus to rescue sinners from the guilt and condemnation of their sins, to give them right standing with Himself now, and eternal glory in the future. That is the gospel—and what a glorious thing it is!

The gospel and the church are to be so intertwined that the latter can't exist without the former. Take the gospel out of the church, and you no longer have a church. You may still have the building, the programs, the leaders, and the public meetings, but those things don't make a church.

We can go further. The Lord has made the church to be a glorious thing, and it is the gospel that makes the church glorious. But if you stand on the front step of your church and wave goodbye to the gospel, you are simultaneously waving goodbye to the glory. If the gospel gets in a car to drive away, the glory of the church gets in the passenger seat and rides along.

What happens when the gospel and the glory depart from the church? I can tell you what ought to happen. There ought to be heart-searching and soul-wrenching prayers of repentance. There ought to be a wholehearted return to the gospel. But oftentimes our response to the departed glory is to act as if it hadn't departed at all. Instead of bemoaning the departed glory, we begin to exalt and magnify things that can never match the glory of what we have lost.

We might say departed glory is the story of humanity. Sinners don't live for the glory of God, and we are all sinners (Rom. 3:23). Lamentably, Christians often fail to live for the glory of God as well. After all, Christians are not perfect. Perfection comes later in heaven.

The good news is that God restores departed glory. He saves sinners through His Son, the Lord Jesus Christ. And when His people fail to live as they should, He forgives them and renews them.

Let's be praying in these days for God to be mightily working in the salvation of sinners and the revival of His people. Let's be praying for a season of glory.

-27-

From God's Word, the Bible...

So Shishak king of Egypt came up against Jerusalem, and took away the treasures of the house of the LORD and the treasures of the king's house; he took everything. He also carried away the gold shields which Solomon had made. Then King Rehoboam made bronze shields in their place, and committed them to the hands of the captains of the guard, who guarded the doorway of the king's house. And whenever the king entered the house of the LORD, the guard would go and bring them out; then they would take them back into the guardroom.

2 Chronicles 12:9-11

Just Call It What It Is!

The story of Ichabod in the previous reading reminds me of another time, decades later, in which a similar thing occurred—the time of Rehoboam.

Rehoboam should have been a spiritual giant. He should have looked at the lives of his grandfather David and his father Solomon and taken note of how God blessed them when they were obedient and chastised them when they weren't.

But if he looked, he didn't take note. Rehoboam was no giant. He was the short man. He constantly came up short. He had a short fuse. He was shortsighted. He fell short, and his kingdom got shortchanged.

In a day reminiscent of the Ichabod day, Shishak, king of Egypt, came to Jerusalem and "took away the treasures of the house of the LORD and the treasures of the king's house" (v. 9). We're also told that Shishak "carried away the gold shields which Solomon had made" (v. 9).

When Shishak packed up his loot and left town, Rehoboam did some things that the author of 2 Chronicles found to be particularly interesting. He, Rehoboam, first replaced the shields of gold with shields of bronze. And then, as if those bronze shields were just as apt to be stolen as the gold ones, Rehoboam instituted a very elaborate system for protecting them. Gold was gone and bronze was beautified. This short man took a shortcut.

We sometimes hear people boldly say of the aging process: "Seventy is the new forty." But everyone who is seventy knows it isn't so. Rehoboam may have been saying: "Bronze is the new gold." But it wasn't. He could act as if those bronze shields were just as beautiful and valuable as the gold shields, but they weren't. And every perceptive Jerusalemite knew things weren't the same. Something of real value had been lost, and what was left was cheap and tawdry in comparison. Perhaps one day as Rehoboam strolled by with his retinue of bronze-bearers, someone shouted: "Bronze is bronze and gold is gold—and this is bronze!"

Despite his attempts to put forward a brave appearance, Rehoboam himself knew the truth of the matter, and "he humbled himself" (v. 12). That humbling caused God to turn away from the wrath that He was planning to bring upon Rehoboam.

Rehoboam steps off the stage of human history as something of a human potpourri—a mixed bag. He humbled himself. That was good. But his epitaph reads: "And he did evil, because he did not prepare his heart to seek the LORD" (v. 14).

Rehoboam speaks to us from his distant day. He shows us how very easy it is for us to substitute bronze for gold, and to become very protective of our bronze. He reminds us that if we had been as protective of our gold as we are of our bronze, we wouldn't have lost our gold.

Individual Christians can repeat Rehoboam's error. We can substitute the bronze of religious busyness for the true gold of communion with the Lord through prayer and the reading of the Word. Yes, let's be busy *for* the Lord, but let's not give that priority over time *with* the Lord.

Churches and pastors can also duplicate Rehoboam's error. In yesterday's reading, I affirmed that the glory of the church is the gospel and asserted that if we lose the gospel, we lose the glory. Today's reading enables us to say the gold of the church is the gospel. If the church loses her gold, she loses the greatest of her treasures. On October 31, 1517, Martin Luther nailed his Ninety-Five Theses to the door of the church in Wittenburg, Germany. The sixty-second of those theses reads: "The treasure of the church is the most holy gospel of the glory and grace of God."

How very easy it is for churches and pastors to become bronze-bearers instead of gold-protectors. And how very easy it is for us to vigorously protect our bronze by saying: "This is a new age. We have to do these things to win people to Christ" (as if people can be won to Christ when Christ is not presented!).

The weighty imperative of this hour is for the church to call bronze what it is and to get back to the gold of the gospel. We can treat our bronze substitutes for the gospel as if they were gold, but that doesn't make them gold. To fail to understand this is to be in company with Rehoboam, and that is not good company to be in.

-28-

From God's Word, the Bible...

And when the people of Ashdod arose early in the morning, there was Dagon, fallen on its face to the earth before the ark of the LORD. So they took Dagon and set it in its place again. And when they arose early the next morning, there was Dagon, fallen on its face to the ground before the ark of the LORD. The head of Dagon and both the palms of its hands were broken off on the threshold; only Dagon's torso was left of it.

1 Samuel 5:3-4

Diving Dagon and His Dense Devotees

The Philistines saw their victory over Israel as a victory of their god, Dagon, over the God of Israel. So, in their Philistine way of thinking, it was only fitting for them to place the Ark in the temple of Dagon as a spoil of his victory

Their smug confidence in the superiority of Dagon got a jolt when the first morning after placing the Ark before him, they found he had fallen facedown before it. It was bad enough that he had fallen, but to fall facedown before the Ark, well, that was particularly embarrassing. If there was ever a time for Dagon to stand in triumph, it was when the Ark was there. But he took a nosedive. Diving Dagon!

We can only imagine how quickly they laid hold of their helpless god and set him back in his place.

The next morning was worse. Dagon had fallen before the Ark again, but this time his head and his hands had broken off! After this second tumble, we might expect to read that one Philistine said: "This really tears it. We can't go on worshipping a god that can't even stand up. Let's throw him on the fire and have a wiener roast!"

If Mr. Perceptive Philistine had been standing there, he would have asked: "Doesn't the fact that Dagon never fell until we put the Ark in his temple not only tell us something about him but also something about the God of Israel?"

But Mr. Perceptive Philistine wasn't there. They were all blind and dense devotees of their diving, tumbling god! In their blindness and denseness they set Dagon up again and declared the place where his head had fallen as a holy place, and they made a rule that no one should step on it (v. 5).

Why did Dagon fall? It was the God of the Ark that made him fall. The supposedly defeated God of Israel was alive and well!

The story of Dagon and his devotees is so comical that we might be inclined to hoot with laughter. But our laughter dies when we stop to wonder if we are in this story. While we don't worship gods that are so patently silly as one that was half-man and half-fish (as Dagon was), we do have our false gods. I would say we have our own trinity—Science, Education, and Government. While these things aren't necessarily wrong in and of themselves, they become wrong when we let them drive God out of our lives. We don't like to admit it, but our gods often fail us. What do we do when they fail? Like the Philistines, we go into our god-propping mode. We set them up again as if nothing had happened. Perhaps the story of Dagon isn't so comical after all!

There can be no doubt that this story contains a powerful indictment of all false gods. But it has an even greater point to make. Wait for that. In the reading on Ichabod, I observed that the glory of the church is the gospel of Jesus Christ and that the church can lose that glory. Yes, sadly enough, the church can lose the gospel!

It's thrilling to me that the account of Dagon comes hard

on the heels of the account of Ichabod. Here's the point we're waiting for—if Ichabod says that the church can lose the glory of the gospel, Dagon says even more forcefully that the gospel never loses its glory. The Israelites had lost the Ark (which was an early picture of the gospel), but the Ark itself had lost none of its glory.

The gospel is under attack these days, and it often appears as if it has been completely defeated. How often the Ark appears to be in the temple of Dagon! But while the enemies of the gospel often celebrate its demise, it has lost none of its saving power. Any sinner who will come to it in repentance and faith will experience that power. And one fine day God will bring this world to an end and will show for all to see the glory of the gospel. On that day, Dagon will fall—never to rise again.

-29-

From God's Word, the Bible...

. . . and declared to be the Son of God with power according to the Spirit of holiness, by the resurrection from the dead.

Romans 1:4

Three Questions with One Answer (1)

Much of our success in living hinges on asking the right questions and on getting the right answers to those questions. Many don't ask the right questions. They go through life without thinking about those things that are truly important. Others ask the right questions only to arrive at the wrong answers.

There couldn't possibly be more important questions than these: Who was Jesus? Can we be right with God? What does the future hold for us? The marvelous thing is that we have the answer to each of these in the resurrection of Jesus.

Think about the first of these questions: Who was Jesus? Is this truly one of life's most important questions? It is. Jesus made the most amazing of all claims. He claimed to be God in human flesh—the God-man! He claimed to be the only one who can provide forgiveness for our sins and give us entrance into heaven (John 14:6).

We must make up our minds about Him. The issues are too great to ignore. If we do choose to ignore them, they don't go away.

The mere fact that Jesus made these claims doesn't mean they are true. There must be evidence to substantiate the claims. So we come to this question: Is there any evidence to support the claims of Jesus? The truth is that there are all kinds of evidence. The words that He spoke, the miracles that He performed, and the prophecies He fulfilled are all very convincing. But the supreme evidence for the claims of Jesus is His resurrection. The Apostle Paul tells us that Jesus was "declared to be the Son of God with power... by the resurrection from the dead...."

The word "declared" comes from a Greek word that referred to the marking off of the boundaries of a field, that is, it referred to something being clearly defined.

Paul says the resurrection of Jesus has clearly declared or defined something, namely, Jesus is "the Son of God with power."

When the Lord Jesus came to this earth as a mere baby, His power and glory were veiled. But when He arose from the grave, the veil was laid aside and He was clearly shown to be what He had been all along—God in human flesh!

Jesus had to be "made" flesh, but He didn't have to be "made" the Son of God. He was already that. All that was necessary was for Him to be "declared" to be God's Son.

How thankful we should be that Paul added the words "with power"! It should go without saying that God's Son would have power. But we oftentimes need to have things spelled out! In Jesus, there is power to save us from our sins, to help us with the difficulties of life, and to raise our bodies from the grave. What power! Let's never forget that He also has the power to judge those who refuse to receive Him as their Lord and Savior.

Paul also tells us that Jesus was raised "according to the Spirit of holiness."

Death is the penalty for sin, but we must not think Jesus died because He was a sinner. The fact that Jesus arose from the grave shows us that death couldn't hold Him. Because Jesus was holy or sinless, death had no legitimate claim upon Him and, therefore, had to let Him go.

Why, then, did He die at all? The answer should thrill us beyond measure. It wasn't because of His sins that He died. It was because of ours! He who knew no sin became sin for us! (2 Cor. 5:21).

God's declaration about Jesus is in. By means of the resurrection, God has declared Jesus to be His powerful, holy Son. Now you, if you haven't already done so, must make your declaration about Jesus. What do you say about Him? Some think they can don't have to say anything about Him, but if we think that, we have already said something. We have said we don't believe Him or accept Him as God's Son. When it comes to Jesus, the wise course is for each of us to say about Him what God the Father has already said.

Who was Jesus? This question has divided the human race for centuries and continues to do so. What is your answer? Have you turned away from sin and are you trusting in Him alone for your salvation?

-30-

From God's Word, the Bible...

Now it was not written for his sake alone that it was imputed to him, but also for us. It shall be imputed to us who believe in Him who raised up Jesus our Lord from the dead, who was delivered up because of our offenses, and was raised because of our justification.

Romans 4:23-25

Three Questions with One Answer (2)

The most important of all meetings lies ahead for each of us. We must meet the God who made us. The date is circled. The clock is ticking. The agenda is set, and it has to do with our standing with God and our eternal destiny! If our standing is right, our destiny is wonderful. If our standing is wrong, our destiny is woeful.

Is it possible to have right standing with God? The grave that Jesus left empty says it is. The Apostle Paul tells us that Jesus was "raised because of our justification" (v. 25).

In other words, Jesus was raised from the grave with the justification of sinners in view. And what is justification? It is right standing with God.

This business of right standing brings us into the legal realm. Here is a man who has run afoul of the law. He fully expects the judge to pronounce him guilty, but, wonder of wonders, he hears the judge say: "Not guilty!"

This guilty man now has right standing with the law. His

relationship to the law is immediately changed by the judge's verdict.

The biblical term "justification" refers to God declaring a sinner to be guiltless. It's God acquitting the guilty. It's the opposite of condemnation.

Isn't it a travesty of justice when a judge pronounces a guilty person to be not guilty? Yes. But that's not what God does with sinners. He doesn't pronounce them "Not guilty" by ignoring their violations of His law. He rather announces that verdict because He Himself has fulfilled all the law's demands on their behalf. How can a perfectly just God let guilty sinners "off the hook"? How can He declare the guilty to be guiltless without incurring guilt Himself?

God's answer is His Son, Jesus. God doesn't just let sinners "off the hook." He has satisfied the just claims of His law against sinners through Jesus. Paul says sinners can "be justified freely" through "the redemption that is in Christ Jesus" (Rom. 3:24).

Jesus lived the life we have refused to live. We incur guilt before God because we break His commandments, but Jesus didn't break any of those commandments. He kept them all perfectly. Then Jesus went to the cross to die a special kind of death. There He actually received the penalty that sinners deserve. Both the sinless life of Jesus and his death on the cross were necessary for sinners to be saved. By his sinless life, Jesus provided for them the righteousness that they didn't have. By his death on the cross, he paid for the sins that they did have. We must never loosen our grip on either of these essential works of Jesus.

How do we know that God has actually done this for sinners through Jesus? God raised Him from the dead! That's the proof of it. By raising Him, God was putting His seal of approval on everything that Jesus did. We must always understand this—God is the One who must be satisfied with what Jesus did to save sinners. How easily we fall into the trap of thinking we are the ones who must be satisfied with Jesus! How utterly wrong that is! God is the aggrieved party, and He must be satisfied.

When Jesus emerged from that grave on the third day, it's as if God sent this triumphant cry resounding through the heavens and echoing through the earth: "I'm satisfied!"

Man pronounced his verdict on Jesus when he nailed Him to the cross. There, evil man cried of Jesus: "He's a fraud!" By raising Him from the dead, God nullified that verdict and announced His own: "He is the Lord and Savior!"

Jesus is the difference between being justified or condemned, but what is the difference between having Jesus and not having him? The answer is in that word "faith" which occurs as a steady, unrelenting drumbeat in the closing verses of Romans 3 (vv. 22, 26, 27, 28, 30, 31).

What is faith? It's resting completely on what Jesus has done. It's resting on His righteousness as our own. It's resting on His death as the payment for our sins. It's coming to the end of ourselves and our own efforts to be right with God and resting completely on Jesus.

-31-

From God's Word, the Bible...

But if the Spirit of Him who raised Jesus from the dead dwells in you, He who raised Christ from the dead will also give life to your mortal bodies through His Spirit who dwells in you.

Romans 8:11

Three Questions with One Answer (3)

Jesus' resurrection powerfully answers three questions. We have examined these—Who was Jesus? How can we have right standing with God?

We come now to this question: What does the future hold for us? Many seem to never turn this question over in their heads. They're only concerned about the here and now. They engage in "nose living," only thinking about those things that are right under their noses.

The Bible constantly warns us that our time on this earth is brief. The death that has stalked us all of our days finally comes. Our bodies go into their graves. Is that the end of them? Or is there more?

In the above verse, the Apostle Paul triumphantly shouts "More!" No, he doesn't actually use the word, but it is definitely the gist of these words: "He who raised Christ from the dead will also give life to your mortal bodies...."

There's more life ahead for these mortal bodies, if—and

what an "if" it is!—"if the Spirit of Him who raised Jesus from the dead dwells in you...."

We are all "indwelt" by something. It could be this world, pleasure, material possessions, fame or influence. The Christian is indwelt by the Spirit of God and by the Spirit of Christ (v. 9), which is, of course, one and the same.

So the resurrection of Jesus guarantees resurrection for all in whom His Spirit dwells.

There are only two classes of people—those in whom the Spirit of God dwells and those in whom He doesn't dwell.

Multitudes would like to believe that the Spirit of God dwells in all without exception. If that were so, Paul wouldn't have said "if."

How does God go about this matter of indwelling us? Paul answers in his letter to the Ephesians: "In Him you also trusted after you heard the world of truth in the gospel of your salvation; in whom also, having believed, you were sealed with the Holy Spirit of promise, who is the guarantee of our inheritance ..." (Eph. 1:13-14a).

What a marvel the Christian is! While he lives in his mortal body, the Spirit of God lives in Him! And while his body is subject to death, his spirit is enjoying life (vv. 10-11). Believers in Christ are in a state of living death. They live spiritually while they are dying physically. But a blessed day is coming when even physical death will be reversed for them, and they will know nothing but life—eternal life!

Pete Seeger's tune *John Brown's Body* has John "a-moldering in the grave." "Moldering" means "turning to dust" or "disintegrating." In pre-Civil War days, John Brown was the man who advocated armed insurrection as the only way to eliminate slavery. John died in 1859. The moldering for John must be complete.

I can't tell you for sure whether John Brown was indwelt by the Spirit of God, but I can tell you that while the Christian's body may completely "molder," it will never molder to the point that it is beyond the resurrecting power of the Lord Jesus Christ.

Unbelievers, on the other hand, are in a state of double death. They are dead spiritually while they are dying physically.

Nothing is more important for us to understand than this: death isn't the same for all. It means one thing for the believer in Christ and something totally different for the unbeliever. The unbeliever's body will also be raised from the grave, but the Bible never calls that a resurrection to more life. It is rather a resurrection unto death (John 5:24-29).

How thankful we should be for the risen Christ! When Jesus sprang from that grave in glorious resurrection life, He answered the greatest questions that the mind can conceive. He answered them decisively. His resurrection declared Him to be God, it declared Him to be the Savior for sinners as it verified and sealed His redeeming work, and it opened the door to all who believe in Him to share in His resurrection. The question now is not whether there are answers to our greatest questions. It is rather whether we will accept the clear answers provided by Jesus.

As we conclude this short section on three questions with one answer, and as this book draws to an end, let me once again urge you to consider how these relate to you and your life. The Lord Jesus Christ is the only hope for sinners and, in His person and work, is the only answer to how a person might be brought into a right relationship with God. Have you in a heartfelt way turned away from sin, and are you trusting personally and exclusively in Jesus as your Savior to deliver you from sin and to bring you safely to His heavenly kingdom?

About the Author

Roger Ellsworth is a retired pastor, active in ministry and writing, who lives in Jackson, Tennessee. He and his wife, Sylvia, love the message of the Bible, and they enjoy sharing the wonderful counsel of the Word of God in language that ordinary people can understand and appreciate.

Roger has written numerous books on the Christian faith, and has exercised a preaching ministry for over fifty years. His sermons are available to listen for free on SermonAudio.com.

The Series

Enjoy collecting the My Coffee Cup Meditations Series.

The "Thumbs-Up" Man 978-0-9988812-5-6 (Series#1)
A Dog and A Clock 978-0-9988812-9-4 (Series#2)
When God Blocks Our Path 978-0-9988812-4-9 (Series#3)
Fading Lines, Unfading Hope 978-0-9996559-1-7 (Series#4)
The Day the Milk Spilled 978-0-9965168-6-0 (Series#5)
"Where Are the Donuts?" 978-0-9965168-7-7 (Series#6)

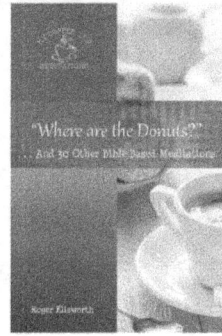

www.mycoffeecupmeditations.com

www.ingramcontent.com/pod-product-compliance
Lightning Source LLC
Chambersburg PA
CBHW070613010526
44118CB00012B/1501